"I read myself along *The Magical Path* and felt myself illuminated from the inside. This book will light your interior lamps and keep them glowing. It's bursting with abundance and practical magic."

— SARK, author and artist of *Glad No Matter What*

"Marc Allen's life is simply successful in every respect. Within these pages he unleashes the magic that has made him a modern-day wizard."

— Isha Judd, author of *Why Walk When You Can Fly?*

"Marc Allen is my role model for easy success. His wisdom is disarmingly simple yet utterly profound. *The Magical Path* is imbued with masterful spiritual truth, edified with many practical examples and applications. I felt nourished and empowered by the well-chosen affirmations. If you practice the ideas and skills this book sets forth, you will find yourself well, successful, and connected to your inner spirit. Read it and come home to all that is good in and around you."

— Alan Cohen, author of
Enough Already: The Power of Radical Contentment

"I can always tell when I have real magic in my hands because all at once I feel relieved, peaceful, and inspired. This is an important book because it offers the tools for living life the way it was meant to be lived — easily, joyfully, and in conjunction with our creative spirit. Every page rings with the truth of a master sharing profound insights divined by innate wisdom and tested by a legacy of successful living."

— William Whitecloud, author of *The Magician's Way*

"Marc Allen is sharing the wisdom of the ages in a way that can guide and coach us to choose and create the life we desire. When we choose life — meaning, what benefits everyone — we unleash an energy and spirit in our lives that creates what is needed for miracles to occur. You will then find your authentic self and personal happiness unrelated to material things. When you choose to be a rebel through kindness and love, you will help to create the true family of man and understand what happiness is."

— Dr. Bernie S. Siegel, author of *365 Prescriptions for the Soul* and *A Book of Miracles*

"Marc Allen deeply recognizes that magic is the discovery of the power we each have to change our lives without having to struggle against life. Marc shows us how we can join with the deep creative flow of life — powerful magic — a flow that unites us with not only what grows and heals us but what supports everyone else as well. I could feel his love for the reader flowing out from his wise teachings. I felt that as much as he loves the subject matter, which he has lived and mastered, he loves those with whom he shares it even more."

— Richard Moss, author of *The Mandala of Being* and *Inside-Out Healing*

"Marc Allen is a living example and proof that the magical approach can help us create our ideal life — easily. The fact that Marc became a millionaire with a wonderful family life, a beautiful home, and a very successful business by using these techniques makes him a very credible expert on the magical approach. His personal journey from poverty to wealth — in an easy and relaxed, healthy and positive way — inspired me to change my belief that success takes hard work and sacrifice. This is a great book for those of us who want to know how to create our dream life with ease."

— Pamala Oslie, author of *Life Colors*

THE
MAGICAL PATH

Also by Marc Allen

BOOKS

The Greatest Secret of All:
Simple Steps to Abundance, Fulfillment, and a Life Well Lived

The Millionaire Course:
A Visionary Plan for Creating the Life of Your Dreams

Visionary Business:
An Entrepreneur's Guide to Success

The Type-Z Guide to Success:
A Lazy Person's Manifesto for Wealth and Fulfillment

A Visionary Life:
Conversations on Personal and Planetary Evolution

The Ten Percent Solution:
Simple Steps to Improving Our Lives and Our World

A Two-Second Love Affair (poetry)

SPOKEN-WORD AUDIO

The Millionaire Course Seminar (3-CD set)

The Spiritual Path to Success (audio download)

Stress Reduction and Creative Meditations (1 CD)

The Success with Ease Complete Course

(12 audio downloads or 12-CD set)

MUSIC

Awakening

Solo Flight

Quiet Moments

Breathe

Petals

THE
MAGICAL PATH

Creating the Life of Your Dreams
and
A World That Works for All

MARC ALLEN

NEW WORLD LIBRARY
NOVATO, CALIFORNIA

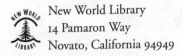

New World Library
14 Pamaron Way
Novato, California 94949

Text design by Tona Pearce Myers

Library of Congress Cataloging-in-Publication Data
Allen, Mark, date.
 The magical path : creating the life of your dreams and a world that works for all / Marc Allen.
     p.   cm.
ISBN 978-1-60868-145-7 (pbk. : alk. paper)
  1. Self-actualization (Psychology) 2. Success. 3. Affirmations. 4. Visualization. 5. Magic. I. Title.
BF637.S4 A5734
133.4'3—dc23   2012024166

First printing, October 2012
ISBN 978-1-60868-145-7
Printed in Canada on 100% postconsumer-waste recycled paper

10 9 8 7 6 5 4 3 2 1

— Dedicated to you —

and to everyone who has taken my courses,

for your love and appreciation

and, best of all, never-ending miracle stories

May we be guided by Spirit

every moment

in our thoughts, words,

and actions.

And miracles will follow miracles,

and wonders will never cease,

because all our expectations

are for the highest good of all.

Contents

2   Affirming the Dream — The Power of the Spoken Word   45

3   Realizing the Dream — The Power of the Written Word   75

4   Magic in a Nutshell — *The Art of True Healing*   95

A Note to Readers

I've sat and pondered, walked around and wondered, whether to write this book in a completely impersonal voice — not mentioning myself in any way, just giving the principles and practices of modern magic — or whether to include the stories from my life, and the lives of others, in a more personal way.

Over the years, a lot of people have told me that the personal stories I tell help them learn to work their own magic more easily, so I've decided to include them — but they're not essential. None of these words are that important — it's what you do with the words that makes all the difference in your life.

If you don't like any parts of this work, skip to another part. There is a vast amount of material here, and not all of it will appeal to everyone. I write in different voices at different times, and you may prefer some voices over others. My daytime writing is very different from the words that drift along in the middle of the night. Don't feel you have to read this whole book straight through. Roam around in it, do a few practices, and find what works for you.

**Take what you need,
and leave the rest.**

When you are inspired

by some great purpose,

some extraordinary project,

all your thoughts break their bonds.

Your mind transcends limitations,

your consciousness expands in every direction,

and you find yourself in a new, great,

and wonderful world.

Dormant forces, faculties, and talents become alive,

and you discover yourself to be a greater person by far

than you ever dreamed yourself to be.

— PATANJALI (ca. 250 BCE)

Introduction

A Magical Path

The magical path is a short path, one that reaches its destination quickly, and for that reason, it's appealing and useful for a great many people, including artists, young people, the overworked, underpaid, overwhelmed, or hopelessly lazy.

The magical path is a direct path to success as you choose to define it. You work directly with the creative forces of the universe, so that the life and the world you picture and focus on in your imagination very quickly become your life and your world in full, three-dimensional reality.

This is a course in real magic.

Real magic exists, absolutely. It is called by many different names by different people all around the world. Whatever word or words you use to describe it, it is the mysterious process by which something is created out of apparently nothing. It is the process that has created this entire vast universe with you and me sitting in it and pondering these words at this moment. It is the ever-mysterious process of life — call it what you will.

I've always liked the word *magic*. I still have memories of the mystery and wonder of childhood, and the word has always fascinated me. You can call it by many other words, including *physics* or *chemistry* if those words seem more accurate or sensible or realistic to you. You can call it *intelligent design* — whatever you call it, however you imagine it to be, there is obviously a vast intelligence within the forces that design and create this universe. You can call it God, you can call it science. You can call it creative visualization. You can call it strategic planning. Successful people use magic all the time, whether they're aware of it or not.

Many people who use magic very effectively don't believe in it, and don't even like the word or the concept of *magic* at all. The word has a great many negative meanings for a lot of people. Yet a large number of them have found out how to apply what we can call the laws of manifestation and — yes — magical creation in their lives. They just give the process different words. Choose whatever words work for you.

The words themselves are not that important — they are tools to summon powers that are far beyond our words. Call this mysterious process anything you want. For the purposes of this course, we'll call it *magic*.

There is an ever-mysterious process of creation;
we can call it many things.
We will never understand how the process works,
but we can consciously set it in motion.

The process begins in the inner world of the mind. It begins with a thought, a dream — something ephemeral, fleeting, as light and vulnerable as a tiny seed blown in the wind. By focusing on that thought, that dream, we can discover how to create it in our lives and our world. We can create something out of apparently nothing.

The course that follows has many different sessions. Each one is an inner journey, and each one is a complete course in itself that contains the essence of this entire course in magic. It is not necessary to master every one of these chapters or even go through this entire course before you will see some expansive changes in your life. Work and play with any one of these chapters, and you'll start seeing some remarkable things happening in your life and in your world.

The important work, the *essential* work, isn't in reading or listening to all these words. It's in the inner journeys you take, and the resulting experiences you have.

A Magical Path in Today's World

It may be helpful to include the story of how I was introduced to magic. It's one example of how the ancient laws and practices of magic can be applied in very simple ways in our lives and world today.

In my early twenties, after three and a half years of college, I was in the worst shape of my life. I had read a great many books and written lots of papers, but I had done little or nothing for my physical and emotional health. I had taken way too many stimulants to get through all the homework and tests, with very little awareness of the harm the drugs were doing to me physically, mentally, and emotionally.

I had periods of depression. As I look back on it now, it's so obvious: What goes up must come down. After several days of taking various stimulants, you're bound to come down. Even worse, perhaps, was the ongoing anxiety I felt so often. Something was wrong with me, I felt, and something was wrong with the world. I couldn't exactly say what it was, but something was messed up, in the world and in my life.

I lived in a state of fear much of the time. One ongoing fear was that I would be overwhelmed with anxiety and depression, and just wouldn't be able to handle it. I had no idea that I could do anything about the emotions that came surging through me. I was powerless on a roller-coaster ride of my own emotions.

As soon as I left college, some remarkable changes happened. I got into a theater company and accidentally started taking a yoga class — the directors felt it was good physical discipline. The physical yoga and meditation we did as a group had a powerful healing effect. In a very short time, I was in much better health.

The yoga and meditation opened me up, in a way, and showed me there were new and different worlds to explore. One time, we did a little practice called *Closing the Gates*, where we sat comfortably, took a deep breath, and then covered our eyes, nose, mouth, and ears with our fingers. (I'll explain in more detail later.) For the first time in my life, I had an awareness of an inner space inside, as vast and broad as outer space.

It sounds odd to me now; it should have been obvious to anyone. But I had never been aware of the fact that we have an inner world, a vast space we can enter at will and explore. A new world had opened up to me — a world of imagination — a world, I discovered soon after, where magical creation takes place.

Not long after I began doing a bit of yoga and meditation (nothing regular, as I was and still am lazy and undisciplined), I wandered into a little bookstore in Madison, Wisconsin. I don't remember the name of it now, but it had something to do with magic, and the entire bookstore was filled with books on magic, East and West. I had never read any of them, never seen any of them. When I entered that bookstore, I entered a new world.

A man with dark hair and a dark beard sat off behind a desk in a far corner. The beard was full and concealed a lot of his face; he could have been in his twenties or his fifties, for all I knew. He read in silence while I wandered around the store. I had an odd feeling, a combination of awe, excitement, self-consciousness, fear, and shock. I had no idea what any of this was about, and no idea where to begin to study the obviously vast and detailed and arcane subject of magic.

I went up to the man behind the desk and asked him where I could begin to learn about this stuff. He smiled, and invited me to sit in an old wooden armchair. Then he stretched back in his chair, relaxed, and began to give me what turned into an hour-long introduction to Western magic.

I left with a load of books under my arm. The shortest one, the first one I read, was *The Art of True Healing* by Israel Regardie. Without consciously thinking about it, I put all the other books aside and just focused on that book. The others sat there for months, years, with barely a glance from me. Over the years, I lost most of them. In Israel Regardie's little book, I found all I needed to work with for many years to come.

The first sentence of the book grabbed and held my attention. It was written simply, with conviction and authority. I had never read any words like them:

THE FORCE OF LIFE

**Within every man and woman is a force
that directs and controls the entire course of life.
Properly used, it can heal every affliction
and ailment we may have.**

And properly used, I soon discovered, it can also help us create fulfilling, successful, wonderful lives. The foundation of the work lies in an exercise of the imagination called the Middle Pillar Meditation. We'll get into it in depth a bit later, but the simple version involves just relaxing and visualizing or imagining that there is a pillar of light that runs down through the center of your body, from the top of your head to the bottom of your feet. That light, that energy, can be directed anywhere, within and without, to heal yourself and others, and also within that field of light are inner worlds of your imagination that can be dreamed, created, explored, and summoned into your life.

The Middle Pillar Meditation is a simple key to magical creation. I started doing the meditation fairly regularly, perhaps a few times a week on average. It took years, because I was young and a complete idiot about many things, including how to make any money doing what I loved. Eventually, though, by doing the Middle Pillar Meditation, I began to clearly imagine the life I wanted to live, and then I started to see that the next steps to take toward creating that life were obvious, and doable, usually quite simple.

One of the little exercises we'll do in the first chapter tricked me into daring to dream of the life I wanted to live *ideally*. Once I got a clear picture of what my ideal life looked like, the next steps I needed to take toward it became obvious. I took one little step at a time, and eventually my dreams were fulfilled, in full-color three-dimensional reality. It all came to be in some mysterious way, in its own perfect time, all by itself.

Over the years, I added a few more things to my magician's toolkit. They were all quite simple, and I can teach them to a ten-year-old — to anyone who is old enough to dream, imagine, read, and write. You don't have to believe me — just try a few of these things, and see what happens.

We were all born with the tools of magical creation in abundance. There is nothing else we need that we don't already have.

The tools of magical creation are simply our dreams and our imagination.

Dare to dream of the life you want to live *ideally*. Then ask your powerful subconscious mind to show you how to create that life in reality.

Ask and you shall receive.

Most of us simply don't ask ourselves the right questions often enough — questions like this: How can I possibly create the life of my dreams? What steps can I take? What plans can I make? When you ask those questions, you start to get answers — and they're the best answers, perfectly tailored to you, because they come from within you.

Ask and you shall receive; seek and you shall find. Jesus wasn't exaggerating when he said that. And he didn't say, "Ask and you shall receive *if you deserve it*." Or if you work hard enough, or have the right education, or if you're lucky, or were born under the right stars. No — he said it simply and clearly, and it is a great key to manifestation: *Ask and you shall receive.*

What are you asking for?

A Word about Repetition

There is a lot of repetition in this course. It is intentional. Repetition is essential. Look at how many times we said and sang the alphabet before we got that down without mistakes — hundreds of times.

Most of us need to read or hear the same material repeatedly before we remember it deeply — deeply enough that it comes to mind, uncalled, when it's most necessary. Deeply enough that it affects our daily lives.

Whenever something is repeated, take it in again and review it. See if it has any new meaning for you. Pay close attention to the physical experience you have while reading or hearing the words over again. Some of these words are meant to be absorbed deeply into your mind and body, reflected on and taken in so that your subconscious mind begins to accept these new instructions and begins to work magic.

Some of the words are printed in bold type and given their own page. I recommend copying some of these and putting them up on your wall. Change any words you wish, and make them your own.

One of the most powerful tools in this course is taking a phrase or prayer that has particular meaning for you and repeating it often, until you've memorized it. When it comes to mind unbidden at just the right moment, then you know that your subconscious is absorbing those words, and you're creating new synaptic pathways, and life-changing miracles are beginning to happen.

You are on your way to creating the life of your dreams.

> **And miracles will follow miracles,**
> **and wonders will never cease,**
> **for all our expectations**
> **are for good.**

The Essence of What I Know

I try to get to the essence of what I know on every page of this book. Maybe, as you read or hear these words, all you'll need is just *one phrase*, and that knowledge — that wisdom — will be enough to launch you into a new world, where you realize your vision, your highest dreams.

Maybe some of you will have an experience like Hui Neng had. He was an uneducated woodcutter who became a great teacher in China over a thousand years ago. He was hauling a wheelbarrow past an open window, and he heard a phrase from a Buddhist sutra being chanted inside the room. He understood that phrase, and was immediately enlightened.

That's all it took — one phrase. That's all it might take for you, just one phrase in all these words. Maybe it's this phrase:

> **The truth is within you.**

It is the intention of this course

to help develop a peaceful army of visionaries,

artists, entrepreneurs, businesspeople,

teachers, and leaders

who are transforming not only their own lives

but the whole world as well,

creating a world that works for all,

in an easy and relaxed, healthy and positive way,

in its own perfect time,

for the highest good of all.

1

DREAM, IMAGINE, CREATE —
THE POWER OF THE WORLDS
WITHIN US

Be at least as interested in what goes on
inside you as what happens outside.
If you get the inside right,
the outside will fall into place.
Primary reality is within, secondary reality without.

— ECKHART TOLLE, *The Power of Now*

Dreams Are Essential

It all begins with a dream. It all begins with a little, ephemeral, vulnerable wish that flits through your mind. Of course — where else can it begin? Everything anyone has ever created first began with a dream.

It begins with an act of courage. Most people lead unsatisfactory lives because they don't dare to dream of an expansive, fulfilled, creative life. Why don't we dare to dream, and why don't we dare to do whatever we can to fulfill those dreams?

The answer is simple: Most of us are filled with fears, and our fears and anxieties overwhelm our vulnerable little dreams. Most of us fear failure so much that it keeps us from doing the things that we really want to do, the things that make us happy, excited, filled with life.

Every successful person in every field will tell you this: Don't fear failure! Don't let your fears overwhelm your dreams. Go for it. You'll never regret it. Yes, you may fail along the way — in fact you probably will. Yet life goes on. Once you fail a few times, you naturally come to realize there's nothing to fear in failure. So you failed — so what? What are you up to now? That's the important thing. This moment is all we have, and we can, in this moment, create some seriously effective magic, if we wish — if we dare to dream.

The Inner World of Imagination

Understanding the power of magic enough so that we can put it to use in our lives doesn't have to be all that complex and difficult. We don't have to join some kind of mystical group and work our way to the thirty-third level of something or other before we can gain a mastery of magic.

It's all very simple, when we think about it:

**Everything that has ever been created
was first created in someone's — or something's — mind.
All creation begins with a thought.**

That's obvious, right? The act of creation starts with a thought, a vague idea, a dream. Where else can it start? It all begins in our imagination.

We have a vibrant world within us. A world of shimmering light, the light of our Presence, our Being (thank you, Eckhart Tolle, for giving us those words). When we explore this world, we discover a world of magical creation. It is where all creation starts: in the inner worlds of spirit and mind.

A lot has been written and said about this. But all those words — and these words — are not that important: It's what you do with the words that affects your life. So let's take a moment right here at the beginning of the course to awaken our imagination, to explore our inner mind, and see what happens. We can begin our journey with the little exercise that, for me, opened up the vistas of my inner imagination.

Closing the Gates

This little meditation exercise is purely optional. If you have done any amount of meditation, you probably don't need to do it. I had done very little meditation the first time I did this, and it had a powerful effect on me.

It's good to start with what is sometimes called the Three-Breath Entry:

THREE-BREATH ENTRY

Sit or lie down comfortably, relax....
Take a deep breath; as you exhale, relax your body....
Take a second deep breath, and as you exhale, relax your mind, let all thought go....
Take a third deep breath, and as you exhale, let it all go....
Deeply relax for a moment....
Feel your Presence...your Being....
Bathe in the light of the life energy within....

CLOSING THE GATES

Lift up your hands and spread your fingers. Now, gently and carefully, put your thumbs in your ears, blocking out as much sound as you can....
Then lay your index fingers over your eyes, lightly, without pressing....
Then take a deep breath, and press your third finger into the side of your nose, blocking your breathing....
Put your ring finger and little finger over your mouth, closing off your breathing there as well....
Sit as long as comfortable, without straining. When you need to breathe, relax your third, fourth, and fifth fingers and breathe through your nose. Keep your eyes and ears closed for a while longer....
There are inner worlds of light within you....

Bathe in the vast shimmering light of the life energy within....

That's it. Maybe it'll have no effect on you at all; maybe you already have access to inner worlds, and it comes as no surprise to look within. When I first did it, I had a stirring experience I'll never forget. I became aware of whole worlds I never knew existed, only because I'd never thought of them before — worlds of pure light, worlds created at the speed of light within the great piece of work we call our mind, our imagination.

You Are a Pillar of Light

The Middle Pillar Meditation is an essential part of my magician's toolkit. It has been one of the few practices in this course that I do regularly, several times a week, even though I'm basically lazy. The great appeal of the meditation is that you can do it lying flat on your back, in my favorite yoga posture — the corpse posture, where you lie motionless, arms at your sides, out at a slight angle, palms up. You can also do it sitting comfortably, or standing, or even walking or running.

Three Versions of the Middle Pillar Meditation

Over the years, I have adapted three versions of the Middle Pillar Meditation, two short and one longer. The first involves just relaxing and imagining that there is a radiant light energy — the energy of life — at the crown of your head, and it flows

down through the center of your body, from head to feet....
That's it — short and simple and sweet.

In the second version, you let the light fill your body while
standing, walking, or even running. The third version is a
longer meditation, with several options. You can change and
adapt any of the versions as you see fit.

Let's look again at the opening words of *The Art of True Healing*:

> **Within every man and woman is a force**
> **that directs and controls the entire course of life.**
> **Properly used, it can heal every affliction**
> **and ailment we may have.**

It can also help us create fulfilling, successful, wonderful,
abundant lives. We are connected at the crown of our heads
with the energy of the universe, and connected at the bottom of our feet with the earth and, beyond that, the whole
universe as well. First, we just imagine a pillar of light energy
shimmering through our body, then we circulate it through
our body, then we direct it. That light, that energy, can be
consciously directed anywhere, within and without, to heal
ourselves and others.

We can also consciously direct that light energy, the light of
our imagination, into the inner worlds of magic, where we
can do all kinds of good things. We can create inner sanctuaries and meet inner guides; we can imagine our highest, most
expansive dreams, and then call forth the energy to create
those dreams in full in our lives and in the world around us.

This simple, relaxed meditation may be all you need to take from this entire course and apply in your life. I highly recommend doing the following exercises. The first two practices don't take much time at all; you can do them in a single moment, with a single breath, any time of day or night.

Simple Middle Pillar Meditation

Take a deep breath, exhale, relax....
Imagine there is a pillar of healing light radiating at the crown of your head....
Feel that light move down through your body, from your head to the tips of your toes....
Then feel it come back up to the crown of your head....
Imagine your body is a single radiant pillar of light....

Imagine you are a pillar of light.

That's the short version. Don't underestimate it. It is a gateway, a portal, that shows us who and what we really are, for we're all filled with the force of life, in every cell of our body. That life, that light, is who and what we are, on the deepest level of our being, now and forever.

Walking Middle Pillar Meditation

As you stand or walk (or even run), feel your Presence within....
Feel your Being....
Your body is a pillar of life energy, bathing you in its healing light....

Yes! Your body is a pillar of light. Feel it within, always....

It is who you are on your deepest level of being....

If you're out at night, you can magnify the experience if you start out somewhere in the darkness and then move into a brightly lit area as you feel the life energy bathing every cell of your body.

For the longer version of the Middle Pillar Meditation, it's always good to start with the Three-Breath Entry.

THREE-BREATH ENTRY

Sit or lie down comfortably, relax....
Take a deep breath; as you exhale, relax your body....
Take a second deep breath, and as you exhale, relax your mind, let all thought go....
Take a third deep breath, and as you exhale, *let it all go....*
Sit for a moment and deeply relax....
Feel your Presence...your Being....
Bathe in the light of the life energy within every cell of your body....

LONGER MIDDLE PILLAR MEDITATION

Take a deep breath, and as you exhale, feel a warm, radiant light at the crown of your head; it is the energy of life....

See it, feel it, vibrant and shining....

Feel it move down from your crown and fill your entire
head — your mind, your third eye — with vibrant
light, peaceful and healing....
Take a deep breath, and as you exhale, relax into this
world of light....

Then feel the light move down again and center in
your throat....
Take a deep breath of air into your throat, and let the
warm light within expand and become a quiet, wonderful healing energy....
Feel the light — it is the warmth of life....

Let it expand again and move down into the center of
your heart....
Breathe warmth and healing energy into your heart
and your lungs....
Let the radiant light expand, and fill the whole of your
being. Let your heart open — open wide — to everyone and everything....

Let that radiant light move down again and center in
your stomach — your *hara*, your third chakra. It is the
center of your power....
Breathe healing light into your stomach, and into the
amazing network of your intestines....
Let the light heal you and empower you....

Let the light move down again and center in your sec-
ond chakra, your sexual organs....
Feel the whole area bathed in warm, healing light....
This energy center is the source of your creativity....

It's where we literally create new life, so fill it with your healing life energy....

Feel it move down finally to your root chakra, right where you sit, and fill that energy center with the healing light of life....

Now let that radiant energy flow down through your legs and out of your feet and into the earth, and into the whole universe....

Let that light energy come up through your feet and up through the central pillar of your body, up to your crown, where it showers over you and bathes your whole body in light....

Do this several times, if you wish....

Imagine your body is a radiant pillar of shining light, connected above with the universe and below with the earth — and beyond, to include everything in this magical creation we call the universe.

Imagine that every energy center in your body is a shining center of light....

They all connect with each other and form a pillar of radiant light....

This light is your essence; this is who you are — light and life.

This light, this life
is who and what we are,
now and forever.
This light, this life is love.

Affirm something like this:

> **Wherever I am, wherever I go,
> my body is a pillar of light.**

Directing the Light Energy

Once you have energized the pillar of your body, from head to feet, there are all kinds of extraordinary things you can do with this focused energy. You can circulate the energy through your body in different ways, and direct healing energy to any part of your body that needs it. You can direct that energy to others as well, and help them heal. You can use it to attract money, resolve problems, and to help out friends with their difficulties.

The ways you can use it are endless. You can use it to magically create what you want in life.

The meditations that follow are suggestions only. Feel free to change them in any ways you wish. (And feel free in general, as well — in life!) I just heard a wise young woman named yvette Soler (that's not a typo — she spells her first name with a lowercase *y*) say that her teacher told her to make at least one change in every meditation or practice she gave her; that way, she makes it her own. Do the Middle Pillar Meditation a few times, and you'll soon be adapting it in all kinds of creative ways.

CIRCULATING ENERGY

Now that you're filled with vibrant, healing light energy, you can circulate it through your body in various ways.

Start with feeling the energy around your feet, radiantly warm....

Imagine it moving up the front of your body, through all the energy centers of your body, moving up through the pillar of light....

It reaches your crown, and then moves down the back of your body, filling you with healing light energy....

Do this as many times as you wish.

Then imagine the energy gathering at your feet again and moving up the left side of your body (or right side, if that feels better), lighting up all your energy centers once again....

It reaches your crown and then moves down the other side of your body....

Circulate this energy a few times throughout your body....

It is the energy of life itself.

Now imagine the energy rises from your feet right through the center of your body, up your shining Middle Pillar....

Every chakra is filled with radiant healing light....

Now the energy reaches your crown and showers over you, down your body, bathing every cell in the radiant healing light of your life energy....

By circulating the light of your life force through your body, you have summoned powerful currents of healing energy into your body. This healing energy is always present in you; now you are magnifying it with the power of your imagination, and directing it with the power of your focused thought. You are ready to heal yourself.

HEALING YOURSELF

Take a deep breath, and relax deeper and deeper as you exhale....
Take another deep breath, and summon radiant life energy....
Let that healing light fill every cell of your body....
Now focus on any part of your body that needs healing, and see it bathed in radiant healing light....
Fill the whole area with light, warm and gentle, radiantly powerful....

Breathe deeply, and breathe oxygen, energy, and warmth into the area....
Relax...and imagine in some way that your body's amazing healing systems are now fully, powerfully engaged, doing their work of healing.

Think or say something like

> **Every day, in every way,**
> **I am getting better and better,**
> **in an easy and relaxed manner,**
> **a healthy and positive way,**
> **in its own perfect time,**
> **for the highest good of all.**
>
> **I am filled with healing energy.**
> **I am healed, I am whole.**
> **I am perfect as I am.**

Sit quietly in the light of your healing presence for a
minute…or an hour, or any length of time.…
Feel your life energy radiating around you, letting
your body's phenomenal healing system do its part.…
Feel yourself healing.…
Tell yourself — affirm — you are healing, you are
whole, you are a perfect creation, filled with life, now
and forever.

Ask and you shall receive. Ask for a healing, then lie down and
give yourself one.

You can heal others as well by the same method. The most
comfortable way is to sit and relax in a chair that's right next
to them. Have them lie comfortably on their back in a bed or
on a couch. If they're open to it, you can go through the meditation together, speaking out loud. Or you can do it yourself,
silently, then speak to them in any way that spirit moves you
throughout the healing.

HEALING OTHERS

Take a deep breath, and relax your body as you slowly
exhale.…
Take another deep breath, and relax your mind.…
Take another deep breath, and let everything go.…
Relax…and feel your presence, your inner being.…
Bathe your whole body in the healing light of your life
energy.…
Circulate the energy for a while, if you feel like it.…

Now take your attention from within and focus it on the person lying before you. Extend the circulation of your energy to include them....
Merge your energy fields into one, so the two of you form one single body of radiant, healing light....

You can simply sit, quiet and motionless, and feel the healing energy at work, or you can raise your hands, and get up on your feet if necessary, and help them amplify their healing energy with your touch.

It's not necessary to touch; you can just hold your hands above any area of their body, and they'll be able to feel the warmth of your presence adding warmth to their presence.

There are all kinds of things you can do with your hands — ask for guidance for what's best in the moment. Here are some suggestions:

Hold your hands above their head, and have them feel the energy in their crown chakra....
Then move down, through all seven chakras and finally through their legs and feet, filling their entire body with healing energy....
Guide them with your hands in circulating the energy in any way that feels appropriate....
Hold your hands, motionless, over any area that needs healing....
Become quiet, and sit with them for a while....

It can all be wordless...or you can say any words that come to you in the moment....

Every day, in every way,
you're getting better and better.

Your body is filled
with radiant, healing life energy.

Imagine yourself healed,
and whole, and strong.
Breathe in the healing energy
of the universe,
and fully activate your phenomenal
healing powers (or systems).

Wherever you are, wherever you go,
your body is a pillar of healing light energy.

You can say a prayer of some kind, if you wish....

I close my eyes and see a field of light.
And I feel that light, and life,
in every cell of my body,
nurturing and healing every cell.
And I know that light, and life,
and love,
is who and what I am,
now and forever.

Amen.

It becomes obvious when you do this kind of healing that it's
highly effective. There was a big study recently that showed
that optimists heal much faster than pessimists, and have a

lot fewer health problems to begin with. There certainly is a power in positive thinking.

There's certainly a power in healing through touch as well. You can feel the energy in your hands; you can feel the energy move through your body and their body as well, and it's obvious this kind of energy helps dissolve stress and aids in healing. This is all perfectly sensible to most people; it's obvious that relaxing and laying your hands on someone will have all kinds of physical benefits.

What strains some people's credulity, though, is when they're told this kind of healing also works at a distance. The other person can be hundreds or thousands of miles away and will still feel the effects of this kind of meditation.

I'm not asking you to believe anything I say at all. I'm simply suggesting you try some of these exercises and see what happens. I never had to come to believe in any of these things, never had to make a leap of faith. I just laid down flat on my back and tried the meditations, and then saw the results.

Shakespeare said it so beautifully, in *Hamlet*:

> **There is far more in heaven and earth**
> **than is dreamt of in your philosophy.**

There is far more in heaven and earth than we will ever understand. There are great mysteries of creation, birth and death, and eternal life that will remain mysteries to us, at least in this lifetime.

We will never fully understand how the process of creation

works — but we can learn how to set that process in motion. The results appear magical to us, and they are magical, because life itself is a magical process.

Don't even try to understand how some of these meditations work — just try them, and see what happens.

HEALING OTHERS AT A DISTANCE

Take a deep breath, and relax....
Take another deep breath, and relax more deeply....
Circulate healing energy through your body....
Do a healing on yourself first, if you wish....
Now think of the person you wish to heal; summon their spirit, their presence....
You don't need to be in their presence to send them healing energy....

Get your bearings, your sense of the four directions, and imagine where they are at the moment on our planet....
Now imagine sending them a brilliantly shining stream of radiant, healing light energy across any distance....
Bathe them in healing light....
Help them with the power of your mind to restore their tremendous natural healing systems....
Pray and affirm....

**Wherever you are, wherever you go,
your body is a pillar of healing light energy.**

**Every day, in every way,
you are getting better and better.**

So be it. So it is.

There are many other ways to adapt the Middle Pillar Meditation to daily use, including attracting money and abundance into your life, helping others, resolving problems, and visualizing your dreams so clearly that you end up realizing them, in an easy and relaxed manner, a healthy and positive way, in its own perfect time, for the highest good of all.

ATTRACTING MONEY AND ABUNDANCE

Take a deep breath, and relax your body....
Take a deep breath, and relax your mind, let all thought go....
Take a deep breath, and *let everything go*....
Just float in the shimmering, healing light of your existence....

Feel that light move through the middle pillar of your body....
Circulate the energy, until you feel fully bathed in healing light....
Now imagine the light around you and within you changing color, and becoming a beautiful, radiant blue....
Blue light attracts, so imagine that light is attracting to you a wonderful stream of all the money and abundance you dream of....

Feel and see yourself showered in the vibrant energy of wealth and abundance....
See and feel it coming to you from any and all directions, north, east, south, west, above, and below....

If you wish, silently or loudly chant the word *El*. It is a name of God....

Visualize, see, feel, sense in some way that the ocean of blue light that fills you is attracting to you all that you wish for.

Every day, in every way,
I am getting better and better.

I live in an ocean of abundance,
light, and love.

So be it. So it is.

HELPING OTHERS

Take a deep breath, and relax your body....
Take a deep breath, and relax your mind, let all thought go....
Take a deep breath, and let it *all* go....
Feel the field of energy within you, healing every cell of your body....

Imagine someone you want to help in some way....
Now imagine the light around you and within you

changing color, and becoming a deep, beautiful, vibrant violet....
Violet light radiates outward, so imagine that light is radiating outward toward the person you want to help....
Imagine their spirit, their presence....
Bring your spirit, your presence, into theirs....
Imagine that your energy can help them, assist them, empower them....
Imagine that you are able to give them what they need, whether it's understanding, or healing, or capability, or abundance, or inner peace, or love, or anything else....

Imagine you are filling their Presence, their Being, with the highest good of your Presence....
Pray and affirm whatever words come to mind....

End with something like:

> **Every day, in every way,**
> **we're getting better and better!**

> **This, or something better, is now manifesting,**
> **in totally satisfying and harmonious ways,**
> **for the highest good of all.**

> **So be it. So it is,**
> **in an easy and relaxed manner,**
> **a healthy and positive way,**
> **in its own perfect time,**
> **for the highest good of all.**

This next one can definitely help resolve some problems that seem difficult, even intractable. It seems to work best when it's done in the middle of the night, when the others involved are asleep.

RESOLVING PROBLEMS

Find a quiet place and time....
Take a deep breath, and relax your body....
Take a deep breath, and relax your mind, let all thought go....
Take a deep breath, and let everything go....
Relax in the healing light of your Presence, your life energy....
Imagine your body is a brilliant pillar of light....
Do as much of the Middle Pillar Meditation as you want....
Circulate energy through your body, if you wish....

Now imagine being filled with radiant healing light....
Now imagine, in the distance, the light of the Presence of the person or people you're having difficulty with....
Feel your Presence draw near their Presence....
Acknowledge the light within them....
One way to do this is to greet them with the word *Namaste*, which means:

I bow to the light within you.

In your Presence, you feel oneness with others....
You feel a loving respect toward all of creation....

Approach them, with loving respect, and talk to them in an imaginary conversation....
Tell them your side of the story, what the problem is as you see it....
Then ask to hear their side of the story....
Listen quietly, and see if you can come to understand their point of view....

Sometimes that's all that is necessary; at other times, you'll want to go on with your imaginary conversation. You can ask them what their ideas are for resolving the problem, what they would like you to do....
Listen quietly and see if they have an answer for you....
Tell them what you would like to see happen that would resolve the problem....
Sit quietly...see what emerges....
A solution may emerge, easily and effortlessly....
A solution that's for the highest good of all....
Affirm:

**Every day, in every way,
we're getting better and better.**

**Our problem is resolved,
in an easy and relaxed manner,
a healthy and positive way,
in its own perfect time,
for the highest good of all.**

So be it. So it is.

Sometimes all that is necessary is to have a brief conversation, and then just leave it until the next day. It might seem as if they've heard what you have said to them in your mind in the middle of the night. You might find that the problem becomes resolved, easily and effortlessly, for the highest good of all.

Your Inner Sanctuary and Inner Guide

The next two meditations were something I learned in a course called Silva Mind Control. They are guided inner journeys, and take us into new worlds — worlds of unlimited imagination.

Start with the Three-Breath Entry, and even add a countdown at the end, if you wish:

THREE-BREATH ENTRY

Sit comfortably, relax....
Take a deep breath; as you exhale, relax your body....
Take a second deep breath, and as you exhale, relax your mind, let all thought go....
Take a third deep breath, and as you exhale, let it *all* go....
Count down, from ten to one, slowly, breathing deeply, feeling like a leaf in the wind, drifting down....
Ten...nine...eight...seven...six...deeper and deeper ...five...four...three...two...one...*zero*....
Feel yourself relaxing into the vast emptiness of all creation....
Sit for a moment and deeply relax....
Feel your presence...your Being....

YOUR INNER SANCTUARY

With your eyes closed, imagine you can see for miles.
...Imagine you can create entire shimmering worlds
in your mind's eye....
Wander through these worlds, moving at the speed of
thought....
Look around until you find your inner sanctuary, that
wonderful place of peace and repose you have within
your mind....
It is a place of total serenity that always awaits you....
It may be a place you've been before — the ocean,
the mountains, the forests, a special place from childhood....Or it may be a place you have never seen
before in this world, a place that exists only in your
imagination, or on some other world....
This is your sanctuary. You are completely safe here.
You feel peaceful here; you are complete here. All is
well....

Add some details — you may see them vividly, or they
might just be wisps of your imagination. What does it
look like? Are you out in nature? Is there a structure of
some kind?
You might even have some kind of inner office here.
Maybe it has a computer you can access. Maybe there
are file cabinets somewhere, filled with any information you need to access....
It is your sanctuary, your place of refuge, and also a
place you can go to for information, knowledge, and
wisdom....

Relax in the light-filled, warm, wonderful sanctuary
you have created.....
Savor your feelings of inner peace.....
Your sanctuary is always here, always available to you,
whenever you need rest, rejuvenation, inner peace,
and answers to your questions.
Any time you spend hanging out here is well spent!

YOUR INNER GUIDE

There is a special guest who comes into your sanctuary
whenever you summon him or her or it: your Inner
Guide.
Your Guide can be summoned simply by your thought
— simply ask to see your Guide, and your Guide will
appear.....
Look in the distance, and imagine that, far away, you
see a tiny figure approaching you.....
As it gets closer, you start to see details. Is it a man?
A woman? A child? An animal? An angel? A saint? A
goddess?
Your Guide approaches you with great love, with radiant warmth.....
Ask what their name is, and listen quietly for the
answer.....
Ask anything you want, and listen.....
Your Inner Guide is always at your call, here to guide
you and protect you and show you the wonder of what
is.....

Sit down and have tea (or a cup of healing elixer!) with
your Guide...or just stand and talk, or dance, or run

around and play, or do whatever you feel like in the moment....

You're creating in your imagination a wonderful inner friend who is always there with great advice and wise counsel. Listen to your Inner Guide....

Thank them for coming. Thank them for their words of wisdom....

Perhaps you embrace....

Your Guide leaves, and you find that, after being in the radiance of their presence, you too are filled with grace, inner peace, and lightness.

When you relax and do these meditations, you see it: the world of shimmering light within you, the light of your Presence, your Being. It is the world of magical creation.

To create anything, you have to imagine its end result, as fully realized as you can. Focus on the end; keep the end in mind. Why not start with the big picture? Why not dare to dream your *ideal* — and explore new worlds with new possibilities?

The Power of Your Ideal Scene

Little did I know, when I was twenty-two, the effect this funny little thing we did would have on me a decade later. I had no idea when I first did it. I'd followed my girlfriend into a back-to-the-land experiment that lasted only about four or five cold and rainy months. But, one night, something happened that I'll never forget.

We were sitting around a fire, maybe ten or twelve of us, and one couple said, "Let's play a game we play at church camp. Let's imagine five years have passed, and everything has gone as well as you can possibly imagine. What would your life look like?"

We went around the fire, and each of us spoke. I have absolutely no idea what I said at the time — so, obviously, it had no effect on my life. But the day I turned thirty, I remembered playing that little game, so I sat down and went through it. The first time I did it, I took a sheet of paper, wrote IDEAL SCENE at the top, and filled the page. It took about ten minutes.

Later on, I did it again in my favorite way: flat on my back, deeply relaxed, starting with the Three-Breath Entry.

THREE-BREATH ENTRY

Sit or lie comfortably, relax....
Take a deep breath; as you exhale, relax your body....
Take a second deep breath, and as you exhale, relax your mind, let all thought go....
Take a third deep breath, and let it *all* go....
Sit for a moment and deeply relax....It feels so good to deeply relax....
Bathe in the light of the life energy within you....

IDEAL SCENE MEDITATION

Become aware of the field of light around you, in front of you, above you, and within you....

Within that shining light, you can imagine anything you want to imagine....

Imagine five years have passed, and everything has gone as well as you can possibly dream. You have become a powerful magician, able to create in reality what you dream of in the scintillating worlds of your mind....

What does your life look like?
What does the world look like?

What do you do on a typical day?
What do you have around you?
What kind of person are you?
What have you accomplished?
What have you given to the world?
What are the most important things in your life?

You are a bright, shining pillar of creative energy....
Your mind and your heart are connected, united....

> **When the worlds you create in your mind**
> **connect with your heart,**
> **you create what you love.**

When the dream you're dreaming in your mind becomes flooded with the love in your heart, it soon becomes manifest in your world....

Imagine your ideal scene, as clearly as you can....
Imagine a life that you love, every moment....

Then surround it in a golden light, and let it go out into the Universe....

Affirm:

> This, or something better,
> is now manifesting,
> in an easy and relaxed manner,
> a healthy and positive way,
> in its own perfect time,
> for the highest good of all.
>
> So be it. So it is.

If you're too lazy to actually do the meditation, here's a short version, a very brief moment of reflection:

SHORT MEDITATION FOR YOUR IDEAL SCENE

Imagine five years have passed, and everything has gone as well as you can imagine. What would your life look like?

Then ask yourself: What can I do to take the next step toward my ideal scene? Listen for an answer, and take the next step.

Taking Care of Yourself and Your World

When you dare to focus on a dream, you can turn that lighter-than-air dream into a concrete goal. The more you focus on it, the more the steps toward it become revealed to you.

When we imagine our ideal scene, it becomes clear to us sooner or later that within our ideal, we take care of ourselves and take care of the rest of the world as well. The two core things to focus on are (1) our own brilliant fulfillment in life, our self-actualization; and (2) a world that works for all. We see that the two things are really one thing, for our lives and the lives of those around the world are inextricably linked. We're one global family sharing the same world.

We all want the same things in life: We all want peace and prosperity. We all want to live in an abundant world that is sustainable for future generations. So we focus on not only taking care of ourselves but making the world a better place as well.

> **Focus on what works for yourself,**
> **and focus on a world that works for all.**

The first step for most of us is to focus on ourselves. We have to take care of ourselves, after all, before we can take care of anything or anyone else.

Make a clear goal of where you want to be in five years, or ten years. Keep the end in mind. Keep focusing on that goal, and the steps toward that goal will be revealed to you.

Along the way, we can have another clear goal to focus on as well: the goal of a world that works for all. Millions of people are already working toward that end. Let's all join them and do what we can to make the world a better place for all.

Let's affirm something like this:

We are now a vital force,
an army of magicians, visionaries, artists,
entrepreneurs, businesspeople, teachers, and leaders
who are transforming not only our own lives
but the whole world as well,
creating a world that works for all,
in an easy and relaxed, healthy and positive way,
in its own perfect time,
for the highest good of all.

So be it. So it is.

2

AFFIRMING THE DREAM —
THE POWER OF THE
SPOKEN WORD

In the beginning was the word,
and the word was with God,
and the word was God....
In him was life;
and the life was the light of men.

— JOHN 1:4

In the Beginning Was the Word

It all begins with a thought, a dream — an ephemeral thing, as we have seen. Then the thought becomes a word, and in doing so, it gains power, momentum, and even substance.

All words have power. Spoken words, written words, even the thoughts in your mind all have power for good or ill — so it's certainly better to focus on the words that bring good into our lives, and let go of the words that bring us harm in any way. That's a no-brainer — and it's not that difficult to do.

> Becoming aware of your thoughts and words
> is a powerful practice,
> a complete spiritual path in itself.

Becoming aware of your thoughts and words can powerfully affect every aspect of your life. For some people, this simple practice is a complete spiritual path in itself. Buddha called it the path of right thinking.

James Allen, in *As You Think*, gave us brilliant insight on the path of right thinking. The book is a little masterpiece, and it is summed up in its opening poem. (In some Buddhist books, it is said that if you can understand the opening poem, you don't need to read the book, because the essence of the book is contained in the poem. I believe that's true of *As You Think* as well.)

> Mind is the master power that molds and makes,
> And we are Mind, and evermore we take
> The tool of Thought, and, shaping what we will,
> Bring forth a thousand joys, a thousand ills.
> We think in secret, and it comes to pass —
> Our world is but our looking glass.

We think in secret, and then we put our thoughts into words. When you focus your words on the good that you want in your life and repeat those words, you amplify their power, and the words become life-changing affirmations. In Eastern traditions, they're known as *mantras*: words chanted and repeated so that their power is amplified.

The word *affirm* literally means "to make firm." When a thought is repeated in silent or spoken words, it becomes more concrete than a fleeting thought. The way affirmations and mantras actually work will always remain a mystery, but we can learn how to set their power in motion. There are many ways to do this, with many different words from different traditions.

Here's one way to look at it:

**Affirmations and mantras program
our vast conscious and subconscious minds.**

Every thought we have and every word we say programs our mind, both our conscious mind and our limitless, powerful subconscious mind. Most of us go through our lives programming ourselves with a great deal of contradictory information, ending up with beliefs that conflict with each other. We dare to dream to some degree, and some of us even tell ourselves that we have the talent and tools necessary to achieve that dream, but we also fill our minds with doubts and fears and beliefs that limit us and eventually can even destroy so many of our dreams.

Affirmations have the power to overcome our doubts and fears, and even to change old limiting beliefs that haven't been serving us very well. Affirmations can replace and change even our most basic beliefs about the nature of our world and of ourselves, and because of this, they can be one of the most powerful tools we have that help us discover a short path to success and fulfillment of our dreams.

I used to believe what many people still believe: Life is basically a struggle. It's hard to succeed. It takes hard work, and a great deal of luck. So few people actually succeed — and those who do are usually miserable anyway. Be realistic: The chances of succeeding are slim — especially for you, with all your problems and shortcomings.

Then somewhere along the way I became aware that *these deep beliefs are not necessarily true in themselves* — there are many people, after all, with completely different sets of beliefs — *but these beliefs become true in our experience if we believe them.* Our beliefs are self-fulfilling. Fortunately, they are pliable, and can and do change.

**Affirmations help us to intentionally,
consciously, change our beliefs.**

Affirm you live in an abundant world, and see what happens. Affirm that you can succeed — as you choose to define success — and even live the life of your dreams, in an easy and relaxed manner, a healthy and positive way, and see what happens. You don't even have to believe in affirmations — just try them, and you'll notice some remarkable changes that happen quickly, even magically.

I've seen my deep, underlying beliefs change dramatically over the years — and I know it was because of the affirmations I kept repeating. My life and in fact the entire world I live in have both changed completely. I now live in an abundant world, where there is no shortage of good.

For years, I struggled with money issues because I believed I was a fool with money, out of control. I just didn't have whatever it takes to be successful. Once I was able to clearly see this belief and express it in those simple words, I was able to come up with an affirmation that completely contradicted it:

I am sensible and in control of my finances; I am creating total success, in an easy and relaxed manner, a healthy and positive way.

I wanted to keep these words in sight, so I wrote the affirmation down in big letters and posted it on the wall in several different places in my home and office. I put a copy of it in my billfold, and another copy by my phone on my desk. I said it a few thousand times over the next few years, and in an effortless, magical way, it became true in my life.

There are a limitless number of affirmations. The best ones are the ones you come up with yourself. Keep adding and changing the words as you see fit.

Affirmations Work

Affirmations work. A vast number of practices from a vast number of traditions work. Prayer works. Declarations work. Mantras work. Summoning works. Creative visualization works. Positive thinking works. Unfortunately, negative thinking also works, and has the power to undermine and destroy our affirmations, prayers, and dreams.

It's as if the whole universe in some mysterious way says "Yes!" to every thought we have. When we affirm something, the universe says "Yes!" — and then starts whispering to us, showing us exactly the next obvious steps to take.

But if our next thought is, "Oh, but it's so hard to succeed, so few people succeed…," the universe says, "Yes, it's hard for you with those thoughts" — and, sure enough, things are hard. It's a struggle. It's tough. It's (to quote a horrible negative affirmation) "one damn thing after another."

T. Harv Eker has a good analogy: It's as if there is a vast universal warehouse, filled with everything our hearts can possibly desire. When we affirm or pray or declare that we are now receiving the things we desire, those words become an order that the universe sets about fulfilling. We will receive the things we're asking for, *unless* our next thoughts are negative or limiting thoughts, doubts and fears, that cancel our order.

We make an order, then cancel it, then make it again, then cancel it again. Our affirmations and prayers come to nothing.

It's worth repeating:

Affirmations work.
Prayer works. Declarations work. Summoning works.
Creative visualization works. Positive thinking works.
Unfortunately, negative thinking also works,
and has the power to undermine and destroy
our affirmations, prayers, and dreams.

But there's hope for every one of us: We can overcome a huge amount of doubt and fear by simply returning to our affirmations, over and over. Post them on your wall, where you'll keep seeing them. Carry some around with you. Read them over and over. Implant them deeply in your mind. And prepare yourself for some inevitable results.

Miracle Story

I've heard countless stories over the years that illustrate the power of the spoken word, affirmations, and mantras. I'm sure you have too, when you think about it.

Just a few weeks ago, I reconnected with an old friend from our back-to-the-land experiment. I hadn't seen her in over forty years, and wanted to hear the story of her life: what she'd been through, where she was now, and where she dreamed of going.

She said she had wandered around through her twenties, much like I had, searching for something or other that seemed to elude her. Then in her early thirties, she read *Creative Visualization* by Shakti Gawain, and she started repeating an affirmation, over and over, through the months and years that followed. These were the words that ended up changing her life:

**I do wonderful work
in a wonderful way
with wonderful people
for wonderful pay.**

After chanting this for a while, some creative ideas, some possibilities, came floating along. She had several ideas she played with, and then one of them started to become much more concrete — more and more details kept coming to mind — until she was able to make a clear, simple plan that felt completely doable. She ended up setting up her own retail store, featuring all of the strange and unusual and wonderful things she loved.

She made a plan and went for it, repeating her affirmation often throughout the day, and for thirty years she had her own business where she did wonderful work in a wonderful way with wonderful people for wonderful pay.

Another Miracle Story

I heard another miracle story recently: Several years ago, a woman was facing bankruptcy and foreclosure on her home; her real-estate career was earning almost nothing after the crash. She had bought her home at the peak of the real-estate bubble, and it was completely underwater — worth far less than the loan. She took one of my seminars and made a list of goals as affirmations in a notebook. Every morning, as she worked out for half an hour on a treadmill or StairMaster, she read her affirmations to herself, over and over.

She affirmed she was paying off her home completely, in an easy and relaxed manner, a healthy and positive way, and she had a million dollars in liquid assets.

Within a few days, she started getting creative ideas. She played with several possibilities that came to mind, but couldn't see how they could work. Within a few weeks, she got an idea that she acted on: working directly with the banks to help refinance homes like hers that were underwater. Within two years, her home was completely paid off, and she had substantial savings — a comfortable nest egg.

She *knows* that the repeated affirmations had an effect, causing the creative ideas to surface in her mind.

There's nothing you have to believe in to make any of this work — just try it, and see what happens.

The Two Most Important Affirmations: The First and the Last

When I look back over the winding path I took from poverty to abundance, it's obvious to me that one of the most powerful, effective things I ever did was to write a list of dreams and goals as affirmations, worded as if they were already coming into being, and repeat those affirmations enough so that my subconscious mind accepted them and went to work fulfilling them.

When I hit my financial low, near bankruptcy, I came up with an affirmation that changed my life and my world:

> I am sensible and in control of my finances;
> I am creating total financial success,
> in an easy and relaxed manner,
> a healthy and positive way,
> in its own perfect time,
> for the highest good of all.

I kept repeating those words, at a time when that affirmation was very different from my current reality — exactly the opposite, in fact. After a few weeks of that affirmation, it began to slowly dawn on me that creating financial success was not all that mysterious, not even all that difficult — and, even better, I began to get all kinds of ideas about how I could actually create financial success in my life.

In the beginning was the word, says John in the Bible. The affirmations you repeat in your mind start to give you ideas — more words in your mind — that show you the steps you can take to build a much more abundant and fulfilled life. And the steps are obvious, simple, and easy to take. In its own perfect time, for the highest good of all, those things you continue to affirm become true in your reality. That's worth repeating....

> **In its own perfect time,**
> **those things you continue to affirm**
> **become true in your reality.**
> **Our subconscious mind knows no limits.**

If we keep telling our subconscious mind we are creating total financial success, it immediately gets to work showing us how to do it. And if we keep saying to ourselves — programming ourselves — that we're succeeding in an *easy and relaxed manner, a healthy and positive way,* our subconscious goes about showing us exactly how to create success with ease.

Make a list of your goals as affirmations. If you don't like the word *goals* for some reason, pick something else, like *dreams.* Repeat your affirmations often enough so that your subconscious mind absorbs and accepts them. You know that's happening when you start getting ideas, seemingly out of nowhere, that show you the next obvious steps to take to move toward your dreams, your goals, your desires.

In the beginning, I had twelve affirmations on my list; the first and the last affirmations are the most important ones. This is what has just naturally come to me, over the years; find your own first and last affirmations, and put them in your own words.

The first affirms my connection with spirit, every moment; it affirms my enlightenment. Yes, we can affirm our way to enlightenment in the same way we can affirm our way to financial success. It all depends on how you define enlightenment, of course. I like to look at it this way:

> **To be enlightened is to realize who we are**
> **and what we are in reality.**

We are, in reality, one with the quantum field, with all that is. We are not our bodies; we are not our thoughts and feelings and perceptions. Those things pass away. We are the eternal force of life that animates our bodies; we are life and light and love itself. That is who and what we are in reality.

Here's the first affirmation on my list — create your own in your own words:

> **In an easy and relaxed manner,**
> **in a healthy and positive way,**
> **in its own perfect time,**
> **for the highest good of all, I pray...**

Spirit flows through me every moment
with its healing energy.
I am guided by spirit, doing God's will.
I offer no resistance to life,
I am at peace with what is,
filled with grace, ease, and lightness.
This is enlightenment.

The last affirmation on my list programs my subconscious mind about other vitally important things in life: family, marriage, friends, and, for me at least, *time alone*. These affirmations are a bit long — I usually just affirm whatever shortened version appeals to me at the moment.

In an easy and relaxed manner,
in a healthy and positive way,
in its own perfect time,
for the highest good of all, I pray...

My marriage and family life and times alone
are filled with grace, ease, and lightness.

I have plenty of time for family and friends,
and plenty of healing time for myself.

This, or something better,
is now manifesting,
in totally satisfying and harmonious ways,
for the highest good of all.
So be it. So it is!

Reflect on these words for a bit, then come up with your own. Words like these can show us a short path to attaining our heart's desires. Their effect can be immediate.

Stress Reduction and Creative Meditations

It has been proven scientifically that spoken words and repeated thoughts have a profound physical effect. Calming words calm your body; aggressive, violent words cause stress and harm your body. Watch what you say! Your whole body reacts to every word.

Listening to spoken words — or silently repeating words in your mind — can reduce stress and help you become much healthier. The right words repeated often enough can help with a great many other things in your life as well, including building wealth and finding fulfillment and self-actualization.

The meditations that follow take about twenty minutes each. You can just do one or the other, or do them together for a deeply relaxing forty-minute journey into the power of creative meditations.

There are several ways you can do the meditations: (1) have a friend read one or both of them to you while you close your eyes and go through the meditation; (2) read slowly through it — take a little piece at a time, then close your eyes and repeat the words to yourself; (3) record it in your own voice, relax deeply, and listen to the recording (one advantage of this is that you can change my words and make them your own); or (4) listen to the recording I have made, titled *Stress Reduction and Creative Meditations.*

Don't underestimate the power of this kind of meditation. When spoken out loud, these words invoke great currents of creative energy. This meditation is one of the few things I have continued to do regularly over the years (mainly because I do it flat on my back, and enjoy the experience so much). I have no doubt the words that follow have had a dramatic impact on my life.

STRESS REDUCTION MEDITATION

Take the next twenty minutes or so for a deep relaxation and stress reduction session. Your body, mind, and spirit will appreciate it.
Take time to get comfortable and enjoy the session; it feels so good to deeply relax....
Find yourself a comfortable chair, or lie down, somewhere you can have twenty minutes of silence, and treat yourself to this deep-relaxation session.

Close your eyes, take a deep breath, and relax your body as you exhale....
Take another deep breath, and relax your mind as you exhale, and let all thought go....
Take another deep breath, and let everything go....
Now count down from ten to one, feeling like a leaf in the wind, sinking deeper and deeper with every count: ten...nine...eight...seven...six...deeper and

deeper...five...four...three...deeper and deeper...two
...one...*zero*....
Sinking down into a level of deep relaxation....
Letting all stress go, letting all tension dissolve....

Take a breath, and relax your feet....
Feel all tension flow out of your feet...let it go; you
don't need it....
Take another deep breath, and relax your ankles....
Let all tension flow out of your ankles, down through
your feet and out....
Take another deep breath, and relax your calves....
Let all tension flow out of your calves and down
through your ankles and out your feet....
Let it go entirely....
Take another deep breath, and relax your knees....
Feel the tension flow out of your knees, releasing and
relaxing....
Let it all go....
Take another deep breath, and as you exhale, let all ten-
sion flow out of your thighs...releasing and relaxing....

Let it all go...you don't need any of it....
Take another deep breath, and let all tension flow out
of your buttocks, releasing and relaxing....
Let it flow down your legs, and out through your feet....
You don't need any of it....
Take another deep, cleansing breath, and let all ten-
sion flow out of your sexual organs....
Let it all release and relax....
Let it go...you don't need any tension.

Take another deep breath, and let all tension flow out of your hips and waist area....Let it all go....
Feel it release and relax....
You don't need any of it....

Take another breath, and feel all tension flow out of your stomach area....
Feel it release and relax....
Feel all tension dissolve, from your stomach down through all of the lower half of your body....
Feel it all relaxing....
Take another deep breath, and let your lower back relax deeply....
Let all tension flow out of your lower back....
Let it go, totally...you don't need any of it....
Take another deep breath, and let your solar plexus relax deeply....
Feel all tension release...let it all go...you don't need any of it.
It feels so good to deeply relax....

Take another deep breath, and become aware of any tension in your heart....
Let go of all stress and tension in your heart...you don't need any of it....

> **This deep breathing is the key to health....**
> **As you inhale, you bring in oxygen,**
> **vitality, life....**
> **As you exhale, you relax and release**
> **all tension and all stress....**

Take another deep, cleansing breath....
As you exhale, let your lungs deeply relax and release all tension....
Feel it all releasing and relaxing....
Take another deep breath, and feel all tension releasing and relaxing in your upper back....
Let it all flow out through your body, so that your whole body, from your upper back down, is deeply relaxed....

Take another deep, cleansing breath...as you exhale, feel all tension in your shoulders releasing and relaxing...completely flowing out of your body....
Let all tension dissolve as you exhale...you don't need any of it....
Take another deep, cleansing breath....
As you exhale, let all tension flow out of your lower neck....
Let it all go....

> **Feel how good it feels to relax
> and release all tension....**

Take another breath, and let all tension flow out of your upper arms, and go down through your arms and out your hands, releasing and relaxing....
Let all tension go...you don't need any of it.
Take another deep, cleansing breath, and let all tension go from your elbows....
Let it all flow out your hands, and let it go....

Take another deep, cleansing breath, and let all tension go from your forearms....
Let it flow out your hands, and let it go....
Release it, and relax it....

Take another deep, cleansing breath....
As you exhale, let all tension flow out of your wrists, and let it go...you don't need any of it....
Take another deep, cleansing breath, and as you exhale, let all tension leave your hands....
Release and relax...enjoy the feeling of deeply releasing and relaxing....
Take another deep, cleansing breath, and as you exhale, feel everything from your neck down releasing and relaxing....
Let all tension go...you don't need any of it....
Let all impurities dissolve....
Let all stress leave your body....
Feel how good it feels to deeply relax...and let yourself be....

Take another deep, cleansing breath, and let the muscles of your face relax....
Feel the tension releasing and relaxing in your face....
Let it all go....
Take another deep, cleansing breath, and let the little sensitive muscles of your eyelids relax....
Let all tension there release and relax....
Let it go....

Take another deep, cleansing breath, and let all tension in the back of your head go....

Let it release and relax....

Take another deep, cleansing breath, and let all tension in the top of your scalp go....

Feel it all dissolving, just floating away....

You're releasing and relaxing as you exhale....

Take another deep, cleansing breath, and as you exhale, feel every bit of tension in your entire body dissolving....

Just let it all go...releasing and relaxing....

It feels very good to deeply relax....

Now roam through your body with your mind...gently and lovingly....

Find if there are any areas of tension...any areas you're holding on to....

If so, take a deep breath, and breathe into them...and as you release that breath, let that tension go....

Let it all go...let your body be completely, deeply relaxed....

You don't need any tension, you don't need any stress....

Let it all go....

Now imagine as your breathe in that you are drawing energy in through your feet and up the left side of your body, up to the top of your head....

As you breathe out, imagine you're running that energy down the right side of your body, from your head all the way down to your feet....

Again, draw it up through the left side of your body....

Imagine that energy cleansing and strengthening your whole body....

As you breathe out, draw it down the right side of your body, cleansing and strengthening and purifying....

One more time — as you breathe in, draw it up the left side of your body...and as you breathe out, draw it down the right side of your body...cleansing, strengthening, and purifying....

Now as you breathe in, draw it up the back of your body, all the way up your back to the top of your head....

As you exhale, draw it down the front of your body, down your face, chest, stomach, legs, all the way down... cleansing, purifying, strengthening, relaxing....

Again, draw it up the back of your body as you breathe in...and draw it down the front of your body as you breathe out....

Bathe in it...enjoy it....

Again, draw it up the back of your body as you breathe in...and let it cascade down the front of your body as you breathe out...all the way down to the bottom....

Now draw it up the center of your body as you breathe in...all the way up the golden energy center of your spine...all the way to the top of your head....

Have it shower over the top of your head, in a beautiful, golden shower of energy that is relaxing, strengthening, rejuvenating, life giving....

Again, as you breathe in, draw that energy up the center of your body, up through your spine, all the way up to the top of your head....

And let it shower over you as you breathe out…bathing you in a shower of light energy….
Again, draw it up…through the power of your imagination, draw that energy up your spine, and out the top of your head….
Let it shower over you, bathing you in golden light energy….

Now just take a deep breath, and as you exhale, relax your body….
Take another deep breath, and as you exhale, relax your mind; let all thought go….
Take another deep breath, and as you exhale, let everything go….
Enjoy your deep relaxation….

It feels so good to deeply relax….

Your body is nurturing itself now…strengthening itself…feeding itself…being good to itself….

Take a few more minutes now to deeply relax….

CREATIVE MEDITATIONS FOR HEALTH, ABUNDANCE, AND FULFILLING RELATIONSHIPS

Now we'll take twenty minutes or so for creative meditations for health, abundance, and fulfilling relationships. As with any of these meditations, feel free to change any of the words to better suit yourself.

Find yourself a comfortable place to sit or lie down, close your eyes, and take a deep breath....
As you exhale, relax your body....
Take another deep breath, and as you exhale, relax your mind, let all thought go....
Take another deep breath, and as you exhale, let everything go....
It feels good to deeply relax....
Now take a breath, and count down from ten to one, feeling like a leaf in the wind, sinking deeper and deeper with every count...ten...nine...eight...seven...six...deeper and deeper...five...four...three...deeper and deeper...two...one...*zero*....
Let all tension go...release and relax....
Enjoy your feeling of relaxation....

Now tune in to your body...feel your body's energy....
Feel life energy coursing through your body...soothing your body...soothing every muscle....
Feel that life energy nurturing your body...cleansing, strengthening....
Imagine your body not as you think it is right now but as you would truly like it to be....
Imagine your body in its total perfection....
Imagine it is strong and healthy...radiant and beautiful...supple and completely pure....
Your body is a perfect servant for you....
It is something to be loved, and admired, and deeply appreciated....
It is something that will serve you well....
Affirm to yourself:

My body is strong and healthy....
My body is strong and healthy....
My body is strong and healthy.

My body serves me well....
My body serves me well....
My body serves me well.

My body is filled with energy....
My body is filled with energy....
My body is filled with energy.

My body is perfectly healthy....
My body is perfectly healthy....
My body is perfectly healthy.

My body serves my purpose in life....
My body serves my purpose in life....
My body serves my purpose in life.

My body is strong and beautiful....
My body is strong and beautiful....
My body is strong and beautiful.

My body is perfect in every way....
My body is perfect in every way....
My body is perfect in every way.

Imagine drawing energy to your body...filling it with
life energy...filling it with strength as you breathe in...
and cleansing and purifying as you breathe out....
Drawing strength and power to you as you breathe
in....

Cleansing all impurities and releasing all disease as you breathe out....
Drawing strength and power as you breathe in....
Letting go of all impurity and all limitation as you breathe out....

My body is my perfect vehicle for my expression....
My body is my perfect vehicle for my expression....
My body is my perfect vehicle for my expression.

My body is my perfect servant....
My body is my perfect servant....
My body is my perfect servant.

My body is in perfect health....
My body is in perfect health....
My body is in perfect health...and I am thankful for it!

Now that we've created a healthy body, let's create a full, abundant life to enjoy....
Imagine as you breathe in that you are drawing abundance into you from all directions....
Imagine as you breathe in that you are drawing abundance to you...drawing energy to you, and recycling that energy out into the universe....
You are drawing abundance to you, and giving off abundantly into the universe....
Imagine that you are drawing all good things to you....
Imagine that you are a channel of good things out into the universe....
Affirm to yourself:

With every breath I take in, I draw in abundance....
With every breath I breathe out, I shower my abundance to all....
With every breath I take in, I take in abundance....
With every breath I breathe out, I shower my abundance to all....
With every breath I take in, I take in abundance....
With every breath I breathe out, I shower my abundance to all.

I live in an abundant universe....
I live in an abundant universe....
I live in an abundant universe.

I am attracting to me all the good that I need....
I am attracting to me all the good that I need....
I am attracting to me all the good that I need.

I see abundance everywhere....
I see abundance everywhere....
I see abundance everywhere.

I deserve to be rich and prosperous....
I deserve to be rich and prosperous....
I deserve to be rich and prosperous.

I am now rich and prosperous, in every way I wish....
I am now rich and prosperous, in every way I wish....
I am now rich and prosperous, in every way I wish.

The more I give, the more that comes back to me....
The more I give, the more that comes back to me....
The more I give, the more that comes back to me.

My very nature is one of abundance....
My very nature is one of abundance....
My very nature is one of abundance.

Every dollar I spend comes back to me multiplied....
Every dollar I spend comes back to me multiplied....
Every dollar I spend comes back to me multiplied.

I use my abundance in all kinds of beautiful ways....
I use my abundance in all kinds of beautiful ways, for
myself and others....
I use my abundance in all kinds of beautiful ways, for
myself and others.

I am rich, and I am free, easily and effortlessly....
I am rich, and I am free, easily and effortlessly....
I am rich, and I am free, easily and effortlessly.

Now that we're healthy and abundant, we will now
create the perfect relationship for us....
Imagine in your mind's eye your perfect relationship....
You may now have that relationship, or maybe you
don't think you do, but imagine that person, or those
persons, with you right now....
You are close, in total harmony and peace... easily and
effortlessly....
Imagine yourself being close to the one you love....
Imagine sharing a deep love with them, and know that
you deserve the relationship that you desire....
Affirm to yourself:

I am now creating my perfect relationship....

I am now creating my perfect relationship....
I am now creating my perfect relationship.

My perfect relationship comes to me, easily and effortlessly....
My perfect relationship comes to me, easily and effortlessly....
My perfect relationship comes to me, easily and effortlessly.

I deserve love....
I deserve love....
I deserve love!

I am love....
I am love....
I am love!

I give love, openly and freely....
I give love, openly and freely....
I give love, openly and freely.

I live in a loving universe....
I live in a loving universe....
I live in a loving universe.

I can communicate my deepest feelings, easily, honestly, effortlessly....
I can communicate my deepest feelings, easily, honestly, effortlessly....
I can communicate my deepest feelings, easily, honestly, effortlessly.

My honesty and my love are the basis of my relationship....
My honesty and my love are the basis of my relationship....
My honesty and my love are the basis of my relationship.

My love and my honesty are now creating my ideal
relationship....
My love and my honesty are creating my ideal relationship, here and now....
My love and my honesty are creating my ideal relationship, here and now.

I give love, openly and freely....
I give love, openly and freely....
I give love, openly and freely.

My love, my openness, and my honesty are now creating my perfect relationship....
My love, my openness, and my honesty are creating
my perfect relationship, here and now....
My love, my openness, and my honesty are creating
my perfect relationship, here and now.

So be it...so it is....

So be it. So it is!

 Repeating words like these when deeply relaxed has an effect
on your mind and body that you can easily feel. Never underestimate the words you think, speak, and write — they have
tremendous power for good or ill.

Let's Make a Pact

Affirm to the world you are on your way, creating the life of your dreams. Find your own words, speak them out loud, and see what happens.

Let's make a pact to repeat affirmations like these:

> In an easy and relaxed manner,
> a healthy and positive way,
> in its own perfect time,
> for the highest good of all,
> I am now creating the life and the world
> of my dreams.

> We are now living and working
> together in partnership
> to create a world that works for all.

> So be it. So it is!

3

REALIZING THE DREAM — THE POWER OF THE WRITTEN WORD

The act of writing is a magical act, able to invoke the powers of creation.

The Act of Writing

It all begins with a thought, a dream — an ephemeral thing, as we have seen. If the thought becomes a word, it gains power, momentum, and even substance, especially if repeated as an affirmation or mantra. If the word is written down, it becomes even more concrete and solid.

When we write down our dreams, goals, affirmations — whether they're scattered all over the place or in a collection in a folder or notebook — we have created our own unique magician's toolkit, and a truly magical thing happens: Our desires turn into intentions. And once you intend to do, be, or have something, there is nothing that can stop you.

**The written word is a powerful device
that can turn desires into intentions.**

The act of writing is a magical act, using symbols we have created on a page to invoke the powers of creation.

I'll first go through the simple steps I took to put my dreams and desires in writing. Then I'll walk you through the steps. They're steps *anyone* can do. And the results are powerful.

The day I turned thirty was the day that changed my life. I took a single sheet of paper and wrote IDEAL SCENE at the top. Then I imagined five years had passed, and everything had gone as well as I could possibly imagine. I dared to dream my *ideal*, the life of my dreams, and put it in writing. All it took was a single sheet. All you need is one or two sheets of paper to create something that can change your life, quickly and dramatically.

I sat with my Ideal Scene for a while, and, even though I was nearly overwhelmed with doubts and fears, I realized that within my Ideal Scene there was a list of goals. I took another sheet of paper and wrote DREAMS AND GOALS at the top and listed them.

Start and build a successful publishing company. (I was a totally clueless poverty case at the time, with no job, no savings, no family support, and no idea how a business operated.) Write a book that has a powerful impact in the world. Record my music. Get into real estate and buy a beautiful home in a peaceful, quiet place. Move deeper into a lasting inner peace. Be as lazy as you want to be. Have fun. My ideal, when I thought it through, was to have success *with ease*.

This process didn't take much time. Writing my Ideal Scene took about ten minutes. Listing my goals took another ten. Within twenty minutes, I had written material that would completely transform my life.

> **Even lazy people
> can create powerful magic.
> It doesn't take a lot of time.**

The next step took maybe fifteen focused minutes: I took another single sheet of paper and wrote **DREAMS AND GOALS AS AFFIRMATIONS** at the top, in big letters, then started with the words *In an easy and relaxed manner, a healthy and positive way, in its own perfect time, for the highest good of all...*

Then I wrote each goal as an affirmation, as if it is now coming into being. *I am now creating...* is a great way to begin. My first goals were *I am now creating a successful publishing company....I am now writing a book that has a powerful impact in the world....I am now recording beautiful music that inspires people to the wonder of what is....I am now finding a home in a beautiful, quiet place....*

Then I added goals that were even more important:

My marriage and family life and times alone are sources of great joy, grace, ease, and lightness....

Spirit flows through me every moment with its healing energy. I am guided by spirit, doing God's will. I offer no resistance to life, I am at peace with what is, and I am filled with grace, ease, and lightness. Every moment, I feel my Being. This is enlightenment.

At first, I had twelve goals; now I'm down to six. I ended with what we call the "Cosmic Insurance Policy":

> ***This, or something better,***
> ***is now manifesting, in totally satisfying***
> ***and harmonious ways, for the highest good of all.***

I promised myself I would read the list every day, but lazy as I am, I managed to actually do it only about once or twice a week, on average. Even so, it didn't take long for those written words to become imprinted in my subconscious mind. I knew the affirmations were having an effect, because plans started coming to mind for each goal, in an easy and relaxed manner.

Over the next few weeks after I first wrote my dreams and goals as affirmations, simple and doable plans just drifted into my mind, and soon I had a one-page plan for every major goal.

I had stumbled on a wonderfully simple form of practical magic. Now let's see how you can try this yourself.

Write Your Ideal Scene

Near the end of chapter 1, we imagined our Ideal Scene. Now we'll write it down:

> Sit down, take a deep breath, and relax your body....
> Take another deep breath, relax your mind, and let all thought go....
> Take another deep breath, and let everything go....
> Relax into the stillness of your radiant life energy....
>
> Stay in this quiet space for a moment....
> Stay in it as you take a single sheet of paper and write IDEAL SCENE at the top.
> Imagine five years have passed, and you've been so inspired by certain brilliant teachers and books and courses that everything has gone as well as you could possibly imagine.
> What does your life look like?
> What is your *ideal scene?*

We begin with the ideal. We begin with the end in mind, and keep it in mind every step of the way. That's the key. Doubts and fears will arise, and will distract us and take us way off our path. When that happens, we just find a way to get back on the path and take the next obvious step in front of us toward the dream, the goal that we keep focusing on in our creative mind.

Put your ideal scene in writing. It's not etched in stone — it can and will keep changing. Keep reviewing it every so often, and make sure it's current. Make sure every word feels right. And be prepared to expand your horizons!

Write Your List of Goals

Sit down, take a deep breath, and relax your body.... Take another deep breath, and relax your mind...let all thought go.... Take another deep breath, and let everything go.... Relax into the quiet stillness of your Being.... You are an ocean of light....

In this quiet space, read your Ideal Scene again. All of your major goals are right there in your Ideal Scene. Take a sheet of paper, and write DREAMS AND GOALS at the top. Now list every goal that comes to mind, every goal you can think of that you want to focus on.

Full disclosure: I have written my list of goals just one time in my life. After that, I rewrote my list of goals as affirmations, and that's the page I have rewritten often over the years; that's the page I carry with me to this day and review often. So let's do it right now:

Write Your Goals as Affirmations

I challenge you to do this little task — it takes about ten or fifteen minutes. I guarantee it will be worth ten or fifteen minutes of your precious time!

Sit down, take a deep breath, and relax your body....
Take another deep breath, and relax your mind...let
all thought go....
Take another deep breath, and let everything go....
Relax into the quiet stillness of your Being....

In this quiet space, take a sheet of paper, and write
DREAMS AND GOALS AS AFFIRMATIONS at the top;
then rewrite each goal as an affirmation, as if each one
is now coming into being, in an easy and relaxed manner, a healthy and positive way....

Sit back and relax again, then read your list of affirmations to yourself, either silently or out loud.
Do this regularly. Whenever you do it, you're focusing
on the end result, and keeping it in mind. Whenever
you do it, you're back on the path of magical creation.

> **Whenever you read your affirmations,
> you're bringing the end results
> clearly into your mind.
> You're back on the short, easy path
> of magical creation.**

Don't worry if you have problems coming up with the right
affirmations right away. Keep working with them, keep reading more and more examples of good affirmations (this book
is full of them) until the best words — the words that feel just
right — are revealed to you.

I could immediately feel the effects of the affirmations when
I first wrote them and then read through them. Those vague,

ephemeral dreams became focused thoughts. The focused thoughts became clearer and more detailed pictures in my mind of the things I wanted to have happen in my life. Those thoughts became even more substantial when they led to making clear, concrete goals — *in an easy and relaxed manner, a healthy and positive way.*

I began to manifest things in my life simply by affirming it was so. My distant, vague dreams became possibilities; the possibilities got clearer in my mind over time, and then some of them started to feel as if — *maybe* — they could be achieved. Some of the dreams started to feel doable, and the next steps to take became obvious.

Somewhere along the way, those vague dreams became clear intentions — and once that happened, they began to manifest, just as I had been affirming. Somewhere along the way, I stumbled across the short, simple path of magical creation.

Write down your affirmations. Carry them around with you. Repeat them often — as often as necessary to make them firm somewhere deep in your subconscious mind. You'll know when it happens because you'll start seeing tremendous changes in your life.

Write Your Plans

Once you start affirming your goals and dreams, plans will naturally start to emerge in your creative mind for each goal. Write these plans down. Keep them short and concise — one page is enough for almost all of your goals.

We want to keep our plans short and simple — written so a child can understand them — because we are working with our subconscious mind as we do this bit of writing. The shorter and simpler our plans are, the easier it is for our subconscious minds to grasp them and accept them.

Once our subconscious minds accept our goals — once the universe says "Yes!" to our plans — we are shown, step by step, exactly how to reach those goals.

> Sit down, take a deep breath, and relax your body....
> Take another deep breath, and relax your mind...let all thought go....
> Take another deep breath, and let everything go....
> Deeply relax into the quiet stillness of your radiant life energy....
>
> In this quiet space, take a sheet of paper, and write one of your goals at the top in big letters....
> Then see what plan emerges from your relaxed, creative mind to achieve that goal....
> What are the most effective strategies you can imagine to reach the goal you're dreaming of?
> Make a short, clear map to success. This little plan is your blueprint.

Don't worry if the plans you come up with at first aren't all that great. They don't have to be remarkably creative or brilliant in order to work, and they don't have to be complete. More will be revealed to you later, as you continue to move

All you need to see is the next few steps to take.

, toward your goal. For now, all you need is a beginning, a very simple plan; all you need to see is the next few steps to take.

The Magician's Toolkit

If you've done some of this writing, you have several pages of notes you'll want to organize in some way.

Find a folder, with pockets on each side. Or put your notes in a special notebook of some kind. When I started, I used a folder with a beautiful picture of misty mountains on it. I wrote, in big words in the middle of the cover, *I am now creating the life of my dreams*. And I signed it at the bottom.

Later on, I added the words *Magician's Toolkit* to the cover of the folder, because I realized that was exactly what I was creating. In your folder or notebook, put all the things you have written so far: your ideal scene, your list of dreams and goals, your list of dreams and goals as affirmations, other things you have already written.

Take the various plans that are forming for your goals, and put each one of them in a separate file folder, so you have a file folder for each major goal as well as your main folder or notebook.

In your file folders, keep your one-page plan on top, then add any other written material you have supporting that particular project.

Create your own magician's toolkit, using your own system and your own words. Keep adding to it, reviewing it, changing and updating the material. <u>This could be one of the single most powerful things you will ever do.</u>

Treasure Mapping

I did some seminars years ago with Shakti Gawain, where we provided drawing paper and colored pens to everyone, along with stacks of magazines, and we invited everyone to draw, cut and paste, and do whatever else they wanted to create a large treasure-map poster.

You fill a poster with visual images of the things you want to do, be, and have — symbols of your successful magical creation. Do it in your own unique way — the variety of the posters created was amazing. The poster is a reminder of the things you want in your ideal scene, the things you want to create in the life of your dreams.

I don't even remember doing one myself — so this little process has had little or no impact on my life — but over the years, I've met so many people who have told me the same remarkable story that I have to include this process here, in this list of powerful magical tools.

Dozens and dozens of people over the years have told me almost the exact same words: They came to one of our workshops, and went home with the treasure map they created. They put it away in a closet somewhere and forgot about it. Five or ten years later, they stumbled across it again, and real-ized *so many of the things on their treasure maps had been real-ized in their lives.*

This process is so effective for some people — probably because it has so many visual components, so many pictures of what you want in life that imprint directly on your subconscious mind — that it only needs to be done once and, even if it's completely forgotten about, it will affect you so deeply in some way that you summon the forces necessary to create what you have pictured.

Posting Quotes

Here's another simple little practice I highly recommend; it's something I do quite often: Whenever you read some words that strike you deeply, words that are obviously true and powerful, words you want to remember and imprint on your subconscious mind, write them or print them out in large letters and put them up on your wall somewhere you will see them often.

Pick a particularly powerful quote and carry it around with you in your pocket, and reflect on it throughout the day. Keep the quotes in sight until you have memorized them. Keep repeating them until you find they sometimes come to mind in the moments when their message is particularly helpful.

This is one of the first quotes I remember putting up on my wall:

**You will become as great
as your dominant aspiration....**

> If you cherish a vision, a lofty ideal in your heart, you will realize it.
>
> — JAMES ALLEN, *As You Think*

When you keep reminding yourself of the truth of words that powerful, those words begin to create subtle changes, and then great changes, in your mind, in your body, in your life.

Writing Down Your Dreams

Write down your dreams, write down the life you want to create, and you discover the power of the written word. Write down any remarkable dreams you have while you're asleep, as well. If you have trouble remembering your dreams, repeat this to yourself just before you're ready to go to sleep: *I will remember my dreams, and their meaning will be clear to me.*

As soon as you wake in the morning, relax, let your thoughts go, and see if you can remember your dream. If it feels like you've already forgotten it, see if you can recall a visual image from near the end of the dream. This has been called "grasping the tail of the snake" — you remember the end of the dream, and then work your way backward, remembering more and more.

Some people say to themselves (and thereby affirm) that they don't remember their dreams. Tell yourself you can and will remember your dreams — and give it a try first thing upon awakening. Be patient, and soon you'll be remembering your dreams. Some of them make no sense (even if we're telling ourselves their meaning will be clear to us); some of them are good therapy, working through and releasing fears and anxieties; and some of them are powerful — even life-changing — messages from our subconscious mind.

Maybe you've already had a life-changing dream you remember. I've had several. About four of them have stayed with me over the years — I keep remembering them, and they continue to bring comfort and inspiration. I'll tell you one of these dreams, because the message of the dream is for you as well as for me.

A Dream That Changed My Life

I was in my early thirties; I had started my publishing company, and it was a mess, on the verge of bankruptcy. Problems followed more problems; I felt a lot of anxiety a lot of the time.

When I look back at it now, I see it from a clearer perspective: My life was a mess because I had a mass of contradicting beliefs that were fighting with each other. Part of me believed that maybe money itself was an evil thing to desire — didn't Jesus say something like that? Part of me felt that maybe these magical rituals I was drawn to do were leading me on the wrong path. I was trying to start a business and had conflicted feelings about the whole idea.

And then, one night, I had a dream:

I was climbing up a mountain. It was filled with boulders and rocks, and the climbing was difficult. Then I came to a path that wound up the side of the mountain. Walking on the path was much easier. Even though I wasn't going directly up, I was working my way up the mountain.

I saw something in the distance: an entrance to a cave that led into the heart of the mountain. I went up to the entrance, and it was blocked by an elaborate gate made of wrought iron. In the center was a tangle of wrought iron, and I played with it a bit and saw it was a puzzle of some kind. I reached in and found a handle — I grabbed it and pulled it out and found it was the handle to a sword. I pulled the sword out of the gate, and the gate opened.

The pathway into the mountain was dark. It kept narrowing, getting smaller and smaller. It was scary — but I had my sword with me. Soon I was on my knees, moving in total blackness through a small tunnel. It turned a corner, and I saw a small door in front of me — just big enough to crawl through. It was filled with golden light.

I got through the entrance and stood up in amazement. The room was a vast cathedral, filled with the light of a million candles — though I couldn't see any light source. The air itself was radiant light. I let my sword fall away — there was no need for it here.

There were three large banquet tables — one near me, one beyond that, and one in the center of the room. I went up to the first table. It was covered with a white cloth that hung to the floor, and it was piled with all kinds of stuff: gold, money, musical instruments, books, little houses, little cars, toys, jewelry, photos, electronic devices, trinkets. And an inner voice said to me, in some way that was silent yet completely clear:

> This is the material plane.
> There is nothing to reject in it.
> It is here for you to master and enjoy!

I stood in silence for a moment, then moved on to the next table. It had a white cloth as well that hung to the floor. There were just four objects on it, neatly arranged: a golden chalice, a large broadsword, a staff with some leaves sprouting from it, and a large golden pentacle — the four symbols on the Tarot deck, the tools the Magician has on his table.

And an inner voice said to me, silently yet clearly:

> This is the astral plane,
> the plane of magical creation.
> There is nothing to reject in it.
> It is here for you to master and enjoy!

I stood in silence for a moment, then moved on to the third table in the center of the vast space. It too had a white tablecloth on it, but it was shimmering with light and looked so insubstantial that you could put your hand right through it. There was nothing on it at all; it just shimmered with its own light.

As I looked at it, an inner voice said:

> This is the spiritual plane.
> There is nothing to attain, nothing to reject.
> It is who you are,
> now and forever.

A force filled with light lifted me off my feet, up into the air, into the shimmering golden center of the cathedral. I spread my arms and felt light pouring through me, from head to foot. I floated in an ocean of light.

I woke up; I was lying on my back with my arms spread wide. I could still feel the light radiating through my body from head to foot. I was motionless for a long time, remembering the dream, knowing the truth of the words, knowing I had been given a great gift.

A great many of my doubts and fears evaporated. There is nothing to reject in the material world; there is nothing to reject in the world of magical creation. They are here to master and enjoy. We are spiritual beings, creations of light and love, and we are here to have a tremendously satisfying and fulfilling physical experience. We are here to create the life of our dreams.

The Power of the Written Word

Keep notebooks handy. Write notes to yourself. Remind yourself of what you know. Put it in your own words. There is a powerful magician and visionary and teacher within you, waiting to be summoned.

Never forget the power of your thoughts and dreams,
the power of the spoken word,
and the power of the written word.

We are endlessly creative beings. It is our nature. We are a part of a vast, endlessly evolving universe. We have the power within us to imagine great things, to dream wonderful dreams. We have the ability to put those ephemeral dreams into spoken words, and turn them into affirmations. We have the ability to write our dreams, affirmations, and plans on paper.

We start with our dreams, and keep asking ourselves how we can possibly make those dreams become the reality of our lives. We list our dreams on paper, and affirm they are coming into being. We end up making plans — concrete, solid plans on paper — and we implement those plans, making changes where necessary.

> We begin as dreamers,
> and then become powerful creative beings.
>
> So be it. So it is,
> in an easy and relaxed manner,
> a healthy and positive way,
> for the highest good of all concerned.

Miracles Will Follow Miracles

I remember the night I realized that I had reached the goals I had written on my list of goals as affirmations — they had been wonderfully, magically fulfilled in my life — and the words *Mission accomplished!* came to mind. Then the next affirmation came along:

> **Miracles will follow miracles,**
> **and wonders will never cease,**
> **because all my expectations**
> **are for good.**

These words sit in a beautiful little glass box, displayed so you can read them through the glass. Those kinds of reminders can and do affect the quality of your life every time you repeat them to yourself.

So be it. So it is.

Magic in a Nutshell —
The Art of True Healing

Within every man and woman is a force
that directs and controls the entire course of life.
Properly used, it can heal every affliction
and ailment we may have.

— Israel Regardie, *The Art of True Healing*

In my early twenties, I conducted a sloppy, disorganized, lazy, and intuitive search through the books of Western magic. Most of the books are vast and complicated. They include systems that take decades to master, and many of them seem to require a committed group of people to work with — in many cases, with a rigid hierarchy of different levels of mastery.

One little book, however, avoids all that complexity. It's a little precious jewel, originally published in 1932, that is the best summary of Western magic I have ever encountered: *The Art of True Healing* by Israel Regardie.

The essence of the book (as we've already seen) is contained in a little exercise called the Middle Pillar Meditation. The very first words of the book give us the tools of magic in two simple sentences: *Within every man and woman is a force that directs and controls the entire course of life. Properly used, it can heal every affliction and ailment we may have.*

And that's not all. *The Art of True Healing* is really *The Art of True Magic*, because it goes on to give us the keys of magical creation in every area of our lives:

> **These are the methods**
> **by which the dynamic nature of the subconscious**
> **can be stimulated so the human personality**
> **becomes transformed into a powerful magnet**
> **attracting to itself whatever it truly desires**
> **or is necessary to its welfare.**

What are these methods, exactly? Very simple and *doable* ones, it turns out. Methods that begin with relaxation and breath, and then engage our creative minds.

The Art of True Healing has obviously affected my life more than any other book on magic. We've already been introduced to it, and it's worth spending some more quality time with it. First, I'll put a few more things from the book in my own words. (I invite you too, to put this and every other thing in this course in your own words.) Then we'll take a good look at the original work.

Awakening Our Energy Centers

It's obvious when we think about it: We have a series of energy centers in our bodies. In *The Art of True Healing*, we focus on five energy centers. In many Eastern teachings, we're given seven. I started using the five-center system, but then changed to the seven energy centers, the chakras, of Eastern thought. Either way is fine — take your pick.

In the five-center system, the energy centers are simply called Spirit, Air, Fire, Water, and Earth. Spirit is at the crown of our heads. Air is the energy between our eyes as well as the energy below that, down to and including our throats. Fire is centered in the heart. Water is the lower belly (the *hara* in Japanese traditions) down to and including the sexual organs. Earth is centered in our feet, and radiates into the earth below.

The seven-center system is a bit different. Each chakra is centered, a hand span apart, from the crown of the head, to the third eye, to the throat, to the heart, to the abdomen, to the sexual organs, to the root chakra at the base of our spine, which connects us with the earth.

We did meditations to awaken our energy centers in chapter 1, and there are more that follow. Most of them involve imagining these centers individually, and then connecting them into a brilliant pillar of light that runs through the center of our bodies.

Why Is It Called the Middle Pillar?

The Middle Pillar Meditation is from the Kabbalah, the tradition of Western magic that is the study of the Tree of Life. (We'll get into this in more depth in chapter 9: "You Are the Tree of Life.")

All creation stems from the Tree of Life. From our perspective, it is upside down, for the roots of the Tree of Life are in heaven. All creation begins on the highest spiritual levels, and then descends into somewhat denser levels of mind, and then emotion, before it finally manifests on the concrete level of physical reality.

Our bodies mirror the whole Tree of Life as well. We are a microcosm reflecting the whole macrocosm: As above, so below. The Tree of Life has three pillars; in our bodies, they are the left side, right side, and center. When we do the Middle Pillar Meditation, we're focusing on feeling the energy coursing through the center of our body, up and down the spine.

An *Art of True Healing* Miracle Story

Not long ago, I was talking to an old friend and got shocking news: His wife had cervical cancer — a cyst the doctors said was probably malignant. They even said there was a 98 percent chance it would be fatal.

As soon as he told me, I asked him if he had a copy of *The Art of True Healing*. He didn't think so, so I immediately emailed him a PDF copy of the book, and rushed a print book to him as well. I told him to sit with his wife, read the beginning of the book, and put his hands over the area needing healing. He began to do so right away.

They went to the doctor two weeks later, and this time, after tests, they were told she had a 50-50 chance of survival. They continued the healing exercises from the book. When they went back to the hospital a week or so later, she was declared completely free of all cancer. Her cyst was benign.

It does no good to deny the power of this type of healing. It does a great deal of good to practice it.

The Art of True Healing

This course wouldn't be complete if it didn't include an in-depth look at the little book that changed my life.

Israel Regardie begins his book without any kind of foreword or introduction. I added a few words as an introduction to the edition New World Library published, and will include some of them here:

Introduction

So much has been written and discussed lately about healing and the mind. The two are of course intricately connected, and understanding about the mind-body connection has merged into the common culture.

Israel Regardie wrote brilliantly on the subject many years ago, and he wrote about the mind-body connection in a way that no one else has written before or since....

The original subtitle describes this book as *A Treatise on the Mechanism of Prayer, and the Operation of the Law of Attraction in Nature*. Though the wording seems a bit bulky by today's standards, the meaning of the words is profound and powerful.

Through the exercises in this book, we turn prayer — or any wish for improvement in our lives or the lives of others — into a powerful instrument for change.

Once you try the Middle Pillar Meditation, once you experience its effects, you will probably agree with me that true magic actually exists — and each of us can be a magician, and a healer, capable of improving our lives and the lives of those we love.

From now on, through almost all of the rest of the chapter, the words are those of Israel Regardie in *The Art of True Healing*. I've indented his words left and right, and added just a few comments, which are not indented. The words are worth reading, rereading, and studying.

In the beginning, he launches right into the essence of the book; his first two sentences directly and powerfully sum up the entire work:

The Force of Life

**Within every man and woman is a force that directs
and controls the entire course of life.
Properly used, it can heal every affliction
and ailment we may have.**

Every single religion affirms this fact. All forms of mental
or spiritual healing promise the same thing. Even psy-
choanalysis and other forms of therapy employ this healing power: The insight and understanding that effective
therapy can bring releases tensions of various kinds, and
through this release the healing power latent within and
natural to the human system operates more freely....

Each one of us has the power to begin the process of
reconstruction for ourselves.

**Each one of us can discover the force
that can bring us true healing
of our bodies and minds....**

By turning the fiery, penetrating power of the mind
inward upon itself, we may become aware of previously
unknown currents of force, currents that are almost elec-
tric in their interior sensation, and that are healing and
integrating in their effect.

It is the willed use of such a force that is capable of bringing health to body and mind. When effectively directed,
it acts like a magnet: It attracts to every one of us who

employs these methods the things that we require or fervently desire or that are needed for our further evolution.

The fundamental, underlying idea of this powerful healing system is this: In the ambient atmosphere surrounding us and pervading the structure of each one of our body's cells is a force, a field of energy. This force is omnipresent and infinite; it is present in the most infinitesimal object as it is in the most proportion-staggering far reaches of the known and unknown universe. This force is life itself.

Nothing in the vast expanse of space is dead. Everything pulsates with vibrant life; even the subatomic particles of the atom are alive.

 The force of life is infinite; we are saturated, permeated through and through with this force, this energy. It constitutes our higher self, it is our link with the entire universe, it is God within us. Every molecule of our physical system is permeated with the dynamic energy of this force; each cell in our body contains it in abundance....

The First Step: Understanding

The first step toward freedom and health
is a conscious realization
of the vast reservoir of energy in which we live
and move and have our being.

When we reflect upon this repeatedly, and make repeated mental efforts to make this part and parcel of our outlook upon life, part of the hard, inflexible shell of the mind breaks down and dissolves. Then, inevitably, life and spirit pour abundantly through us. Health spontaneously arises, and a new life begins as our point of view undergoes this radical change.

Moreover, it appears that we create an environment in which we attract just those people who can help in various ways, and the things we have longed for manifest in our lives.

The first step is a purely mental one, involving a change in our perception of life, so that we realize we are in the midst of a vast reservoir of healing energy.

The Second Step: Rhythmic Breathing

The second step involves learning a process of regulated breathing — quite a simple process, and, as you will see, quite an effective one when used repeatedly....

Sit comfortably, or lie down, flat on your back, in a perfectly relaxed state. If sitting, the hands may be folded in the lap, or they may rest comfortably on the thighs, palms upward. If lying down, your hands should rest comfortably at your sides, palms upward.

Let the breath flow in while mentally counting very slowly, one...two...three...four....Then exhale, counting the same beat.

It is fundamental and important that we should maintain the initial rhythm we have started, whether it be at a four-beat count or a ten-beat count or any other count that is convenient. For it is the very rhythm itself that is responsible for the easy absorption of vitality from without, and the acceleration of the divine power within.

Unchanging rhythm is manifest everywhere in the universe. It is a living process whose parts move and are governed in accordance with cyclical laws. Look at the sun, the stars, and the planets. All move with incomparable grace, with a steady, inexorable rhythm. It is only humankind that has wandered, in its ignorance and self-complacency, far from the divine cycles of things. We have interfered with the rhythmic process that is inherent in nature. And how sadly we have paid for it!

**Through quiet, rhythmic breathing,
we can attune ourselves once more
to the intelligent power that functions
throughout nature.**

Our periods of rhythmic breathing can be at any time of the day or night when there is little likelihood of disturbance.

We should cultivate above all the art of relaxation: Learn to address each tensed muscle from toe to head as you sit in a comfortable chair or lie flat on your back in bed. Tell it deliberately to loosen its tension and cease from its unconscious constriction. Think of your blood flowing copiously to each organ in response to your command, carrying life and nourishment everywhere, producing a state of glowing, radiant health.

Begin your rhythmic breathing, then add this preliminary exercise, slowly and without haste. Gradually, as the mind accustoms itself to the idea, the lungs spontaneously will take up the rhythm. In a few minutes it will have become automatic. The whole process then becomes extremely simple and pleasurable.

It is difficult to overestimate the importance or effectiveness of this simple exercise. As the lungs take up the rhythm, automatically inhaling and exhaling to a measured beat, they communicate it and gradually extend it to all the surrounding cells and tissues. Just as a stone thrown into a pond sends out widely expanding ripples and concentric circles of motion, so does the motion of the lungs.

In a few minutes, the whole body is vibrating in unison with their movement. Every cell seems to vibrate sympathetically. And very soon, the whole organism comes to feel as if it were an inexhaustible storage battery of power. The sensation — and it *must* be a sensation — is unmistakable.

Simple as it is, the exercise is not to be taken lightly or underestimated.

It is upon the mastery of this very easy technique that the rest of this system stands.

Master it first. Do it enough times so that you can completely relax and produce the rhythmic breathing in a few seconds.

The Energy Centers

There are five major spiritual energy centers. Since we must name them and identify them in some way, let me give them the most noncommittal and noncompromising titles imaginable, so that no system of prejudice may be erected upon them. For the sake of convenience, we may name the first one Spirit, and the succeeding ones Air, Fire, Water, and Earth.

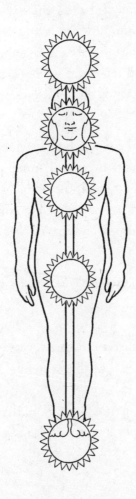

The diagram illustrates the position and location of these centers. It is important to understand that these centers are not physical in nature and position — though there are parallels with our physical organs and glands. These organs exist in a subtler emotional or psychic or spiritual part of our nature. We may even consider them, not as realities themselves, but as symbols of realities — great, redeeming, and saving symbols.

Under certain conditions we may become aware of them in very much the same way that we may become aware of different organs in our physical bodies. We often speak of reason being situated in the head, emotion in the heart, and instinct in the belly; there exists a similar natural correspondence between these centers and various parts of the body.

There are three principal means for us
to become aware of these centers,
and awaken them from their dormant state
so that they may function properly.
The means are *thought*, *sound*, and *color*.

First, through our thoughts, we concentrate on the assumed position of these centers, one by one. Then we make the sound of certain names, which are to be considered as corresponding vibratory rates to be intoned and vibrated. Finally, each center is visualized as having a particular color and shape.

The combination of these three things gradually awakens the centers from their dormant states. Over time, they become stimulated, each functioning according to its own nature, and they pour forth into the body and mind a stream of energy and power.

Ultimately, when their operation becomes habitual and stabilized, the spiritual power they generate may be directed by will to heal various ailments and diseases both of a physical and a psychological nature. It can also be communicated to another person by a quiet, focused laying on of hands. And by simply thinking, with intent and focus, the energy can also be communicated from mind to mind telepathically, or transmitted through space to another person miles away — for objects in space cause no interruption or obstacle to its passage.

The Middle Pillar Meditation

First of all, the centers are to be stimulated into activity while either sitting upright or lying down flat on the back in a perfectly relaxed state, just as we did earlier in the preliminary exercise.

If sitting, the hands may be folded in the lap, or they may rest comfortably on the thighs, palms upward. If lying down, your hands should rest comfortably at your sides, palms upward. Calmness of mind should be induced, and several minutes of rhythmic breathing should result in the sensation of a gentle ripple playing over the diaphragm.

Then imagine there is a ball or sphere of brilliant white or golden light above the crown of your head. Do not force the imagination to visualize the sphere of light, for this only results in the development of neuromuscular tension, and defeats our end. Let it be done quietly and easily. If the mind wanders, as indeed it will, wait a moment or two and gently lead it back.

At the same time, vibrate or intone a sound. You have several choices here:

(1) You can simply hum a pitch that seems to resonate, as closely as possible, in the light of your center. Or you can resonate the pitch in your throat center, and direct it mentally to the center of your choice.

(2) You can intone the word from the Judeo-Christian mystical tradition that is appropriate to that particular center. For the first center, the word to vibrate or intone is *Eheieh*, pronounced *Eh-heh-yeh*. (We'll discuss these words in more depth in a moment.)

(3) You can chant an English equivalent of the ancient word. For the first center, the words to chant are *I am*.

(4) You can meditate upon each center, and discover the words or sounds that have power and meaning for you.

I'll have to insert a comment here: At first I played with several of these suggestions, but as time went on, I let the sound go and just focused on the light energy in the various centers. The sound is not critical to success, nor is imagining words in the various energy centers. If you're comfortable doing some kind of sound, by all means do so, and it'll make the results that much more powerful. But sound is not necessary; I've done this meditation in total silence for many years, and have seen remarkable results!

Also, he directs us to "let the mind rest" in the various centers for five minutes or so — that would mean twenty-five minutes for this part of the meditation. I take much less time in each center; sometimes even just a single breath when I want to move on to other parts of the meditation, such as circulating the force, healing, or attracting abundance.

> After a few days of practice it will become quite easy to imagine the name vibrating above the head in the so-called Spirit center. This name, this center, is the indwelling and overshadowing divinity in each one of us, the basic spiritual self that we can all draw upon. *Eheieh* means literally *I am*, and this center represents the *I am* consciousness within.

> The effect of mentally directing the vibration to the Spirit center is to awaken the center to dynamic activity. Once it begins to vibrate and rotate, light and energy are felt to emanate downward upon and into the body. Enormous charges of spiritual power make their way into the brain, and the entire body feels suffused with vitality and life. Even the fingertips and toes react to the awakening of the coronal (Spirit) sphere by a faint prickling sensation at first being felt.

> If you're intoning a word or a name rather than humming a pitch, the word or name should be intoned during the first few weeks of practice in a moderately audible and resonant tone of voice. As skill is acquired, then the vibration may be practiced in silence, the name or words being imagined and mentally placed in the center. If the

mind tends to wander, the frequent repetition of the vibration will greatly help concentration.

Let the mind rest in the light of the Spirit center for five minutes or so. Let it glow; feel its dynamic energy. Then imagine that it emits a white or golden shaft downward through the skull and brain, stopping at the throat. Here it expands to form a second ball of light, which includes a large part of the face, up to and including the eyebrows.

We name this sphere the Air center, and a similar technique should be applied to this center as to the previous one. It should be strongly and vividly formulated as a pulsing sphere of brilliant white or golden light, shining and glowing from within.

The name that should be vibrated here is *Jehovah Elohim*, pronounced as *Yeh-hoh-vah Eh-loh-heem*. Or you can use the words *I see, I speak*. Or meditate upon that center, and make up your own words. Or simply hum into that center's radiant light.

The traditional names for the centers — *Eheieh, Jehovah Elohim*, and so on — are in reality the names ascribed in various parts of the Old Testament to God. The variety and variation of these names are attributed to different divine functions. When acting in a certain manner, God is described by the biblical scribes by one name; when doing something else, another name is used, one more appropriate to the actions or states of being that are represented or described.

This system has its roots in the ancient Hebrew mystical tradition. Its innovators were obviously people of exalted religious aspirations and genius; their work transcends time and even all the wide varieties of religious and philosophical beliefs.

For our purposes, no religious connotations whatsoever are implied by the use of these biblical divine names. Anyone may use them without subscribing in the least to the ancient religious views, whether he or she be a Jew, Christian, Hindu, Buddhist, Muslim, someone who worships in an indigenous way, an atheist, or anything else.

This is a purely practical, empirical system that is successful regardless of the skepticism or faith of the operator. Today we may consider these sacred names in an entirely different and useful light: They are keynotes of different components of our nature, doorways to so many levels of that part of the psyche that is usually subconscious.

They are vibratory rates or symbolic signatures of the psychophysical centers we are describing. Their use as vibratory keynotes awakens into activity the centers with which their rate is in sympathy, and conveys to our consciousness some recognition of the many levels of the subconscious spiritual side of our personalities. The actual religious significance of these names does not concern us, nor do their literal translations.

Let us focus again on the Air center in the throat, and let the vibratory sounds be intoned a number of times, until their existence is recognized and clearly felt as a definite sensory experience. There is no mistaking the sensation of its awakening.

About the same length of time should be spent here, and in the following centers, as was devoted to the contemplation of the Spirit center. Once this period of time has elapsed, let it, with the aid of the imagination, thrust a shaft of light downward from itself.

The light descends to the solar plexus region, just beneath the sternum or breastbone, and the shaft expands once again to form a third sphere. This is the position of the Fire center.

The allocation of fire to this center is particularly appropriate, for the heart is usually associated with the emotions, with love and the higher feelings. The diameter of this sphere should extend from the front of the body to the back.

The name to vibrate here is *Jehovah Eloah ve-Daas*, pronounced *Yeh-hoh-vah Eh-loh ve-Dah-ahs*. Words to vibrate here are *I love*.

Take care that the intonation vibrates well within the white or golden sphere. If this is done, a radiation of warmth will be felt to emanate from the center, gently stimulating all the parts and organs around it.

Since the mind functions in and through the body, being coextensive with it, the mental and emotional faculties likewise become stimulated by the dynamic flow of energy from the centers. The seemingly solid barrier between our conscious and subconscious minds — an armored partition that impedes our free expression and hinders spiritual development — slowly begins to dissolve. As time goes on, and the practice continues, it may disappear completely and the personality gradually achieves integration and wholeness.

Genuine health spreads to every function of mind and body, and happiness follows as a permanent blessing.

Continue the shaft downward from the solar plexus to the pelvic region, the region of the generative organs: the Water center. Visualize here, too, a radiant sphere of approximately the same dimensions as the higher one. Intone here, too, a name that produces a rapid vibration in the cells and molecules of the tissue in that region: *Shaddai El Chai*, pronounced *Shah-di El Chi* (the *ch* is guttural, as in "loch"). The English words to intone here are *I create*.

Let the mind dwell on the sphere and the words (or the pure vibration, if you choose) for some minutes, visualizing the sphere as a white or golden brilliance.

Each time the mind wanders from such a brilliance, as in the beginning it is bound to do, let it gently be coaxed back by repeated and powerful vibrations of the name or words or tone you associate with the center....

The final step is to visualize the shaft descending once more from the reproductive sphere, moving downward through the thighs and legs until it strikes the feet. There it expands and forms a fifth sphere. We have named this one the Earth center.

Let the mind visualize here exactly as before a brilliant, dazzling sphere the same size as the others. Vibrate the name *Adonai ha-Aretz*, pronounced *Ah-doh-ni hah-Ah-retz*, or use the words *I bless*.

Spend several minutes awakening this center by fixed and steady thought and by repeated intonation, then pause for a short while.

**Try to clearly visualize the entire shaft
of silvery or golden light,
studded as it were with five gorgeous diamonds
of incomparable brilliance.**

Visualize the entire shaft, stretching from the crown of the head to the soles of the feet. A few minutes is usually enough time to give reality to this concept, and bring about a vivid realization of the powerful forces that, playing upon the personality, are eventually assimilated into the physical, mental, and emotional system after their transformation and passage through the imaginative centers.

The combination of rhythmic breathing with the willed visualization of the descent of power through the light shaft or Middle Pillar, as it is also called, produces by far the best results.

Adding Color

As skill and familiarity are acquired in the formulation of the centers, an addition to the technique may be made. Earlier I remarked that color was an important consideration in this technique. Each center has a different color attribution, though it is wisest for a long period of time to refrain from using any other color than white or gold.

To the Spirit or coronal center, the color white or gold is attributed. It is the color of purity, spirit, divinity, and so on. It represents, not so much a human element, but a universal and cosmic principle overshadowing the whole of humankind. As we descend the shaft, however, the colors change.

Lavender is attributed to the Air or throat center, and it represents particularly the mental faculties, human consciousness as such.

To the Fire center, red is an obvious association.

Blue is the color ascribed to the Water center; it is the color of peace, calmness, and tranquility, concealing enormous strength and virility. In other words, its peace is the peace of strength and power rather than the inertia of weakness.

Finally, the color ascribed to the lowest center of Earth is russet, the rich, deep color of the earth itself, the foundation upon which we rest.

Each of these centers has an affinity or sympathy with a different spiritual component. One center is sympathetic to or associated with the emotions and feelings, while another has a definite intellectual quality. It follows logically, therefore — and experience demonstrates this fact — that stimulating these centers and gradually bringing them into a state of balance and equilibrium evokes a sympathetic reaction from every part of our nature.

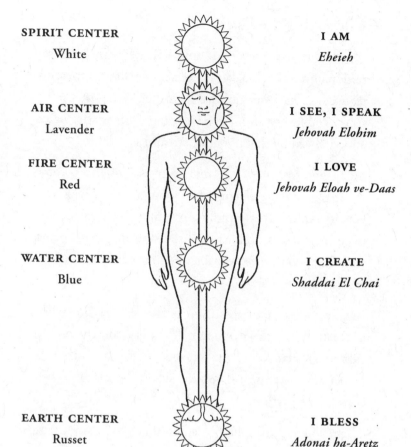

| SPIRIT CENTER | | I AM |
| White | | *Eheieh* |

| AIR CENTER | | I SEE, I SPEAK |
| Lavender | | *Jehovah Elohim* |

| FIRE CENTER | | I LOVE |
| Red | | *Jehovah Eloah ve-Daas* |

| WATER CENTER | | I CREATE |
| Blue | | *Shaddai El Chai* |

| EARTH CENTER | | I BLESS |
| Russet | | *Adonai ha-Aretz* |

Where disease is manifesting in the body, the activity of the appropriate center must be considered as affected somehow in an unhealthy way. Its stimulation by thought, sound, and color tends to stimulate the corresponding psychic principle and thus disperses the maladjustment. Sooner or later a reaction is induced physically in the disappearance of the disease, and the consequent building up of new cells and tissues: the manifestation of health itself.

Circulating the Force

Having brought power and spiritual energy into the system by means of visualizing the centers, how best are we to use it? That is to say, use it in such a way that every single cell, every atom, every organ becomes stimulated and vitalized by that dynamic stream?

To begin, we throw the mind upward to the coronal sphere again, and imagine it to be in a state of vigorous activity. It revolves rapidly, absorbing spiritual energy from the space around it, and transforming it in such a way that it becomes available for immediate use in any human activity.

Imagine, then, that this transformed energy flows like a stream down the left side of the head, down the left side of the trunk and the left leg. While the current is descending, the breath should slowly be exhaled to a convenient rhythm.

Then slowly inhale, and imagine that the vital current passes from the sole of the left foot to the right foot, and gradually ascends the right side of the body. In this way it returns to the source from which it was issued — the coronal center, the human source of all energy and vitality — establishing a closed electrical circuit.

Visualize this energy flowing within the body rather than traveling around the periphery of the physical body. It is an interior psychic circulation rather than a purely physical one. Once the circulation is firmly established by the mind, let it flow evenly to the rhythm of your breathing for some seconds so that the circuit has been traversed about half a dozen times — or even more, if you wish.

Then repeat it in a slightly different direction. Visualize the vital flow as moving from the coronal center above the head down the back of the head and body. It turns forward under the soles of the feet and ascends up the front of the body in a fairly wide belt of vibrating energy. This should also be accompanied by a slow, steady exhalation and inhalation of breath, and should continue for at least six complete circuits.

The general effect of these two movements is to establish in and about the physical form an ovoid shape (shaped somewhat like an egg) of swiftly circulating substance and power. Since the spiritual energy dealt with by this technique is extremely dynamic and kinetic, it radiates in every direction, spreading outward to an appreciable distance.

It is this radiation that forms, colors, and informs the ovoid sphere of sensation, which is not limited to the shape or dimension of the physical frame. General perception and experience has it that the sphere of luminosity and magnetism extends outward to a distance more or less identical to the length of the outstretched arm. And it is within this aura, as we may call it, that the physical person exists rather like a kernel within a nutshell.

Circulating the force admitted into the system by these mental exercises is tantamount to charging it to a considerable degree in every aspect of its nature with life and energy. Naturally this is bound to exert a considerable influence, so far as general health is concerned, upon the enclosed "kernel" within.

The final method of circulation resembles the action of a fountain. Just as water is forced or drawn up through a pipe until it jets up above, and falls in a spray on all sides, so does the power directed by this last circulation.

Now throw the mind downward to the Earth center, and imagine it to be the culmination of all the others, the receptacle of all power, the storehouse and terminal of the incoming vital force.

Then imagine that this power ascends, or is drawn or sucked upward by the magnetic attraction of the Spirit center above the crown of the head. The power ascends the shaft until it surges overhead with a marvelous fountainous display and falls down within the confines of the ovoid aura.

When it has descended to the feet, it is again gathered together and concentrated in the Earth center before it surges up the shaft again.

The fountain circulation should accompany a definite rhythm of inhalation and exhalation. By these means, the healing force is distributed to every part of the body. No single atom or cell in any organ or limb is omitted from the influence of its healing, regenerative power.

Healing

Once the circulations are completed, let the mind dwell quietly on the idea of the sphere of light, spiritual and vital and healing, surrounding the entire body. This visualization should be made as vivid and as powerful as possible.

The sensation following the partial or complete formulation of the aura in the manner described is so marked and definite as to be quite unmistakable. It is marked by an extreme sense of calmness and vitality and poise, as though the mind was placid and still.

The body, completely at rest, feels in all its parts thoroughly charged and permeated by the vibrant current of life. The skin over all the body feels a gentle prickling and warmth, caused by the intensification of life within. The eyes become clear and bright, the skin takes on a fresh, healthy glow, and every faculty — spiritual, mental, emotional, and physical — becomes considerably enhanced.

If there are any functional disturbances in any organ or limb, this is the moment when the attention should be directed and focused on that part. The result of this focus of attention directs a flow of energy over and above the general equilibrium just established. The diseased organ becomes bathed in a sea of light and power.

Diseased tissue and diseased cells, under the stimulus of such power, become gradually broken down and ejected from the personal sphere. The revitalized bloodstream is then able to send to that spot new nourishment and new life so that new cells, tissue, fiber, etc., can easily be built up. In this way, health is restored by the persistent concentration of divine power.

When this is carried on for a few days in the case of superficial ailments, and for months in the event of chronic and severe troubles, all symptoms may successfully be banished without others coming to take their place.

**There is no suppression of symptoms;
the result of these methods
is elimination of the disease.**

Even mental and emotional problems may be effectively dealt with by using these techniques, for the currents of force arise from the deepest strata of the subconscious mind, where mental and emotional neuroses have their origin — where they lock up our natural energy, preventing spontaneous and free expression of the psyche. The upwelling of vital forces through the entire system dissolves the crystallizations and armored barriers that divide the various strata of psychic function.

Where physical disease is the problem to be attacked, the procedure to follow is slightly different — and, if the problem is serious, one should still of course consult a competent physician. In this instance a considerably stronger current of force is necessary in order to dissolve any abnormalities, such as growths or lesions, and to set in motion the systemic and metabolic activities to construct new tissue and cellular structure.

To fulfill these conditions, it is ideally very helpful to have a second person to assist, so that his or her vitality may be added to that of the sufferer in order to overcome the condition. Here is a useful technique — one that my experience has discovered to be supremely successful, and one that anyone can adopt:

First of all, completely relax every tissue in the body before attempting the Middle Pillar technique. The patient is placed in a highly relaxed state by first simply becoming aware of every neuromuscular tension. Consciousness is then able to eliminate tension and induce a relaxed state of that muscle or limb.

Spinal manipulation and massage, with deep kneading, is very useful to begin with, for in this way an enhanced circulation of the blood and lymph system is produced — and, from the physiological point of view, half the battle is won.

Once a suitable degree of relaxation is obtained, the patient's feet are crossed over the ankles and the patient's fingers interlaced so that they rest lightly over the solar plexus. The operator or healer then sits on the right side of the person if the patient is right-handed (and on the left for a left-handed patient) and places his or her right hand gently on the solar plexus under the patient's intertwined hands, and his or her left hand on the patient's head (these are reversed for a left-handed patient).

A form of rapport is established at once, and within a few minutes a free circulation of magnetism and vitality is set up, easily discernable by both patient and healer.

The patient's attitude should be one of absolute receptivity to the incoming force — this will naturally occur if the patient has unwavering confidence and faith in the operator's integrity and ability. Silence and quiet should be maintained for a short while; then the operator silently focuses on his or her own body and performs the practice of the Middle Pillar, still maintaining physical contact with the patient.

The healer's awakened spiritual centers act on the patient by sympathy.

A similar awakening is introduced within the patient's sphere, whose centers eventually begin to operate and throw a stream of energy into his or her system. Even when the operator does not vibrate the divine names audibly, the power flowing through his or her fingers sets up an energy that produces healing activity within the patient, whose psycho-spiritual centers are sympathetically stirred into the active assimilation and projection of force so that, without any conscious effort on the patient's part, his or her sphere is infused with, even invaded by, the divine power of healing and life.

When the operator arrives at the circulation stage, the operator employs his or her visualizing faculty — a veritable magical power indeed — so that the augmented currents of energy flow not only through his or her own sphere but through that of the patient as well.

The nature of their rapport now begins to undergo a subtle change. Whereas formerly there existed close sympathy and a harmonious frame of mind, mutually held, during and after the circulations there is an actual union and interblending of the two energy fields. They unite to form a single continuous sphere as the interchange and transference of vital energy proceeds.

The healer — or the healer's subconscious psyche or spiritual self — is able to divine exactly how strong the projected current should be, and precisely where it should be directed.

A number of treatments incorporating the cooperation and training of the patient in the use of these methods should certainly go far in alleviating the original condition. If necessary, medical and manipulative methods may usefully be combined with the methods described to facilitate and hasten the cure.

Although I have stressed healing of physical ills, it cannot be insisted upon too strongly that this method is suitable for application to a host of other problems. This technique will be found to be a powerful creative tool in all other situations that may arise, whether it be a problem of poverty, character development, social or marital difficulties — in fact, any type of problem one has....

Perhaps sickness is present. Or we need money. Or we have undesirable moral or mental traits — or whatnot.

We can elevate our minds
by utilizing this energy,
so that the desire of our heart
automatically realizes itself
with practically no effort at all.

Magic in a Nutshell

Those are what I consider to be the essential words in Israel Regardie's *The Art of True Healing*. It's one of the shortest books on magic ever written, and one of the most powerful. Even just the condensed version we have seen in this chapter can be looked at as an entire course in magic in itself.

And the Middle Pillar Meditation is so enjoyable to do as well, which is why I've continued to do it over the years. You can do it on your back, completely relaxed. (Full disclosure: I fall asleep quite often when I do this meditation — often enough that it's become a joke in my family every time I say I'm going off to meditate. "Yeah, right," they say, and then they make loud snoring sounds. It's true I sometimes snore when doing this meditation, but sometimes I have wonderful, powerful journeys of the imagination — journeys that have changed the course of my life.)

You can adapt the Middle Pillar Meditation in an infinite number of creative ways. You'll find you just naturally enjoy the process — it's a great excuse to be lazy, after all — and your enjoyment in itself becomes part of the powerful force of creation that the meditation unleashes.

Spend some time enjoying your visualization, whatever it may be, so you feel deeply, emotionally, exactly how it feels to do, be, and have what you want in your life.

**If what you want is in alignment with
your highest good — your spiritual being —
if you have a clear idea of what you want to create,**

**and if you envision it regularly enough,
it will soon manifest for you in physical reality.**

End your meditation with whatever feels comfortable and appropriate for you: You can let your visualization float off into space, and let the universe take care of the details; you can say a prayer; you can imagine the whole planet bathed in the healing light of your radiant meditation; you can meditate quietly, bathed in the light of your inner radiance, watching whatever thoughts arise, and letting them go; you can ask for guidance in your life, and listen for answers from the deep sources of wisdom within you; or you can simply sit, or lie on your back, in wonderful, healing silence.

Finish with a final deep breath, open your eyes, and come back into waking reality, feeling relaxed, refreshed, peaceful, in harmony with yourself and your world.

So be it. So it is.

5

The Prayer of Protection, Magical Circles, and Pyramids

There are only two ways to live your life.
One is as though nothing is a miracle.
The other is as though everything is a miracle.
I choose the latter.

— Albert Einstein

All life is a miracle, because the force of life itself is a miracle. Your body is a miracle. Your mind is limitless. There are more connections in one square millimeter of your brain than there are stars in the Milky Way. That means we all have the capability to be endlessly creative. It means every one of us is a magician — if we choose to look at it that way.

The Prayer of Protection

One of the best tools in our magician's toolkit is the Prayer of Protection. Repeating these words — or similar words — is powerful. While saying this prayer, you can focus on yourself, or you can encircle others in the light of your prayer. You can do it for your family; you can do it for the whole earth.

There are many different forms of this prayer. Some don't have the words *flows through me, and heals me*. As always, find the words that feel best to you.

> Sit or lie down comfortably. Or stand quietly.
> Take a deep, relaxing breath, and as you exhale, let all thought go....
> Feel your Presence...it is the life energy within....
> Say the prayer silently to yourself, or whisper it, or proclaim it loudly to the world:

The light of God surrounds me,
The love of God enfolds me,
The power of God flows through me,
And heals me, and protects me.
Wherever I am, God is,
And all is well.

The light of God surrounds us,
The love of God enfolds us,
The power of God flows through us,
And heals us, and protects us.

**Wherever we are, God is,
And all is well.**

God is present everywhere, so wherever you are, God is. And where God is, all is well.

Another way to say it: The force of life is present everywhere. And where the force of life is, all is well.

These are powerful words to repeat, many times throughout the day if necessary. When Brazilians meet and greet, the typical first words are, "Tudo bem?" "Tudo bem." *All is well? All is well.*

So be it. So it is.

The Magical Circle

Many magical traditions employ the creation and use of a magical circle. There are many ways to create one; find whatever works best for you. Some involve just simple, momentary visualizations; some involve more elaborate imaginings or even physically marking out a circle on a floor in some way.

The essence of creating a magical circle is simply to imagine, whether standing, sitting, or lying down, that your body is surrounded by a circle. Within that circle is the entire world, the entire universe.

As above, so below.

A tiny bit of the whole is a microcosm that reflects the whole macrocosm.

You can quickly create a magical circle around you at any time, using the power of your imagination. You can do it instantly, or you can walk around in a circle, and clearly define it in your mind.

The options of what you can do in a circle are as limitless as you are. You can use it for prayers of protection and cutting cords of attachment. You can draw to yourself, summon, any and all energies you want or need.

You can do every meditation we've done so far in this course within your circle. You can use it to help you create the life of your dreams.

Being in a magical circle can unleash powerful creative energies, and even destructive energies, if you're ignorant enough to go down that road. Before we get into any specific practices, I'll say just a few words about white and black magic at this point. This is the only time in this course we'll even bother to mention black magic.

Magical ritual can be used for good or for ill. Obviously, anyone who uses it for ill — to harm any other person — is stupid, and is badly misusing the power of magic, because they only end up hurting themselves. Anyone who goes into black magic does not understand the inexorable law of karma. Whatever you do comes back to you. Anyone who tries to hurt another person ends up hurting themselves.

When I was first introduced to magical circles, I was given a valuable bit of advice. Magic works on what is sometimes called the astral plane — a word used to describe the plane of imagination, the plane of emotion, thought, and spirit that transcends the physical plane.

The astral plane has two aspects: the higher and lower. All our work, all our focus, should always be on the higher astral plane, for it's filled with the light of compassion, expansive strength, and wisdom. The lower astral plane is filled with the darkness of anger, greed, and ignorance, and should be avoided completely. Don't go there. You will only hurt yourself.

> **The mind is its own place, and in itself**
> **Can make a Heaven of Hell, a Hell of Heaven.**
>
> — JOHN MILTON

The things we focus our minds on become the reality we create. We can choose whether to create a heaven or hell in our lives, here and now. The choice is up to us.

There is a simple way we can avoid creating any problems as we work with magic — something we've already seen several times in this book: We keep affirming that everything is done for the highest good of all. We never choose to harm anyone or anything. We end our sessions with:

> **This, or something better,**
> **is now manifesting,**
> **in totally satisfying and harmonious ways,**

for the highest good of all.
So be it. So it is.

Now we're ready to create our magical circle, knowing it will only be of great benefit, knowing it will never bring harm to anyone.

CREATING A MAGICAL CIRCLE

You can stand, sit comfortably, or lie flat on your back. Close your eyes, and take a deep, healing breath, and relax your body....

Take another deep, healing breath, and relax your mind, let all thought go....

Take another deep, cleansing breath, and let everything go....

Relax for a moment in the stillness and wonder of what is....

Open your eyes, and clearly imagine the boundaries of a circle that surrounds you....

Imagine you are in the center of the circle....

If you wish, and if you're able to, you can walk around the perimeter of the circle several times, in a clockwise direction, clearly defining the size and placement of the circle....

It's not necessary to physically walk around the circle; you can do it in your mind, focusing your attention around and around the circumference of the circle, in a clockwise direction....

Do this several times, until you feel contained in a circle of light, a luminous pillar of energy....

Close your eyes, and put all your attention within this luminous circle....

Within this circle is a microcosm reflecting the macrocosm of all that is....

Within this circle is the entire world, and the whole universe....

The thoughts you have and the things you do here in the center of the circle affect the whole universe....

It's good to start with the Prayer of Protection, if you wish....

You can draw to yourself, summon, any and all energies you want or need....

You can cut any cords of attachment that are limiting your dreams in any way....

Do any of the meditations we've done in this book, and their effects will be amplified by the focused power of a circle....

> **If you can imagine it clearly enough,**
> **it can become a reality,**
> **in an easy and relaxed,**
> **healthy and positive way....**
>
> **Clearly imagine the life of your dreams....**

SUMMONING

With the power of your imagination, you can call forth the presence, the spirit, of any person or animal or divine being you wish....

Here are a few possibilities; pick what works for you.

Imagine Jesus is standing in front of you....
His arms are spread out wide, and he is filled with
radiant love, immersing you in wave after wave of
healing energy....
You are summoning the spirit of Jesus, and it is love,
love, love....
Talk to him, if you wish....
Ask for what you want.

Ask and you will receive.

Imagine Mary spreading her arms out to you....
Her heart is filled with compassion and love for all....
Her radiant peace protects you and heals you and fills
you with radiant peace within....

Imagine anyone you wish from any tradition that
comes to mind and heart....

Imagine Buddha sitting in front of you....
He radiates the light of the great wisdom that comes
from understanding the nature of reality....
He radiates peace, grace, and lightness....
He *is* light, and so are you....
Feel the radiant energy of the awakened one....
It is your energy as well....
It is pure light....

Imagine Buddha turns a deep sky blue, and becomes
the Healing Buddha....
Bathe in the ocean of the shimmering healing energy
of the universe....

Imagine your Inner Guide coming to you....
She, he, it approaches you from a distance, then comes
close, filling you with radiant energy....
Talk with them — they have exactly the right advice
for you in this moment....

Imagine a teacher you've met....
It could be a spiritual teacher, or it could be any kind
of person you want to become....
By simply remembering them, you are summoning
their energy, you are bathing in their Presence....
It is called *darshan* in some Eastern traditions, the
wordless teaching of being in the presence of someone
enlightened....
Let your inner teacher guide you....

**The best guidance we receive
is from within.**

Let your own spontaneous creativity take it from
there....

Summon the spirit of anyone you wish....
Imagine him/her/it in front of you....
Call them forth in your mind's eye....
And you will be in their Presence....
It's always for the highest good of all....
And all we need to do to keep making sure of that is to
keep repeating the words:

**This is for the highest good of all.
So be it. So it is.**

Remembering

We do a form of summoning all the time — we call it remembering. If it's someone we love, it has one effect on us. If it's someone we're having a problem with, it has another effect.

Remembering is a wonderful, simple, powerful practice when done consciously rather than unconsciously. What teachers have you had, what people have you met, who have an energy that comes from being at a higher level of consciousness? By remembering them, you can draw into their Presence, and move into a higher level of consciousness.

I'll never forget my Zen teacher, Katsuki Sekida. Every time I think of him, a smile comes to my face — I remember the grace, ease, and lightness of his presence, and I relax and enjoy the moment. His presence merges with my presence, and I become much lighter.

(I still study his book, *Two Zen Classics*, with his commentaries on the koans, the short teaching stories of various Zen masters over the years. The koan I've been pondering for many months now is this: The master asks, *How can you be free from life and death?* Katsuki Sekida's entire commentary: *How can you be free from life and death? Don't worry about it.*)

In the past decade, I've been informally summoning the spirit of Eckhart Tolle as well. It's exactly as it is when I think of my Zen teacher: As I remember the playfulness, the understanding and love in his face, a smile comes to my face, and I relax and enjoy the moment.

Sometimes a quote from him will come along:

> **To offer no resistance to life
> is to be in a state of grace, ease,
> and lightness.**
>
> — ECKHART TOLLE, *The Power of Now*

Just repeating those words can summon grace, ease, and lightness into our lives.

It's far better for us to spend less time summoning the people we're arguing with or struggling with and spend more time summoning the people who bring us grace, ease, and lightness.

Who brings a smile to your face? Keep calling them to mind, and you'll be smiling a lot more. Who touches your heart? Who makes you a better person? Who has what you want to have?

Summon them; remember them. Open your heart and mind to those who can lead you to more expansive places. We're naturally doing it already; let's do it more consciously, picking the best things to focus on and letting other things go.

This is a powerful tool for conscious evolution.

Cutting the Cords of Attachment

As we interact with people in our lives — and as we do any kind of summoning — we form subtle but sometimes strong connections with those people. If that person is a friend or lover or teacher who touches our heart, these connections are wonderfully healing. These are the connections to cultivate.

But if it's someone we're struggling with in some way, or someone whose presence makes it more challenging to pursue and realize our dreams, those connections can become cords of attachment that are not serving us in any positive way.

There is a simple ritual that cuts the cords of attachment to anyone:

> Walk around in a circle, clearly defining it in your mind....
> Stand in the center of the circle, facing north.
> Raise your arms up fully, stretching them up above your head, so your fingers are reaching high, pointing to the heavens....
> Then turn your hands so your palms are facing toward you, and sweep both arms down in front of you, making a cutting motion with your arms. (Your right arm moves counterclockwise, your left clockwise.)
> Do it as fast or as slow as you wish....
> Imagine you are cutting off all links of attachment that are in any way binding, constricting, inhibiting....
> You are freeing yourself from any limiting or negative influence of others, and summoning your own light, your own power....
>
> Sweep the cords of attachment three times facing north; then three times facing east, three times facing south, and three times facing west....
> Turn in any direction, and let your awareness drift upward....
> Feel the crown of your head....

Feel the pillar of light that descends through you when you summon it in your mind....
You are that pillar of light....
You are filled with light and life and love....
You are love.... Fill yourself with love....
End with the Prayer of Protection, if you wish...or just end by feeling that ocean of love and light within you....

There are times to connect with each other, and times to stand alone in our circle, influenced only by the life energy of the universe....

Creating a Mandala

Mandala is a Sanskrit word that means "circle." In Hindu and Buddhist traditions, a lot of sacred art is in the form of a mandala. The basic form of most Hindu and Buddhist mandalas is a square with four gates, one on each side, containing a circle within it and a center point. From that basic form, many other forms of mandalas have evolved.

Just as in the magic circle, whatever mandala you choose, and whatever you choose to be in the mandala, represents — and even contains — the entire world, the entire universe. You can create a mandala from anything you wish. It can be an altar of some kind; it can be objects and designs you put on a shelf or a small table. It can be a single object; it can be a design on the floor.

There are an endless number of beautiful pieces of art, both traditional and nontraditional, that are mandalas. Traditional Tibetan mandalas often have a pyramid mountain at the center: Mount Meru, the center of the universe.

Creating a mandala is powerful. It's very much like creating a magic circle. Your thoughts, prayers, affirmations projected onto a mandala or repeated within a mandala become amplified in some mysterious way.

You don't have to believe this is true; all you need to do is find or create your own mandala, give it some attention and energy, and see what happens.

That's true for any ritual or exercise in this book. As I've said before, and will say again, you don't have to take a leap of faith to accept that these things can have an effect in your life. Just try a few of them, and you'll start to see some results, some remarkable changes, in your life and your world.

The Pyramid of Human Consciousness

It's good to have a pyramid somewhere, on your mandala or altar. Visualizing or imagining a pyramid in various ways is another powerful form of active meditation.

You find pyramids in magic traditions all over the world. They represent several different things, including the center of the universe and the power of spirit to manifest on the physical plane — from a tiny perfect point at the top to a large, substantial base. They can also represent levels of human consciousness.

There are many different ways we can look at the pyramid of human consciousness. I've found two over the years that have been valuable to visualize: the Eastern and the Western versions, if you will.

Some mandalas in Eastern traditions have a pyramid in the center, representing the center of the universe as well as the pyramid of human consciousness — every level of humanity, from those at the bottom whose lives are based in fear, anger, and violence to those at the top who have discovered abiding light in their lives, inner peace, enlightenment.

A common Tibetan *thanka* — a painting, usually on silk — has the pyramid of Mount Meru in the center and, when you look closely, it has dozens of different colored horizontal stripes going up to the top, each with a different label. The stripe at the bottom is bright red. My Tibetan teacher pointed at it and said simply, "Murderers."

Committing murder takes you to the lowest level of human consciousness. The ascending levels correspond to the seven energy centers, or chakras, within the human body, which are also levels of consciousness: Those on the bottom are dominated by fear, anger, violence, greed, frustration, suffering, and endless unfulfilled desire.

We move up the pyramid of consciousness by awakening the higher energies in our bodies — the energies of love and compassion in the heart center, creative expression in the throat,

inner vision in the mind, and, above all, the wisdom of ultimate understanding.

The essence of the process was summed up concisely in *A
Course in Miracles*: There are two basic states of consciousness, two basic emotions, at the root of all our behavior: love
and fear. When we are dominated by fear, we find ourselves
trapped in the lower levels of human consciousness. It is only
love that can overcome our fears, for love causes us to move
into the higher levels of consciousness, culminating in self-
fulfillment and self-realization.

A Pyramid Meditation

Sit (or lie on your back) comfortably....
Take a deep, relaxing breath, and as you exhale, let all
thought go....
Feel your Presence....
Feel the life energy within you....

Imagine your body is a pyramid....
If you're sitting, imagine being enveloped in a shining
golden pyramid with the peak above the top of your
head....
If you're lying down, imagine your body is part of the
base of a great pyramid of light....
The top of the pyramid rises above you; the peak of
the pyramid is high above you....
If you're lying down, it is centered over your heart....

Imagine radiant light emanating from the top of the pyramid....

It fills the crown of your head, your third eye, your throat, and your heart with light, life, and love....

It awakens the highest centers of your body....

It is the highest wisdom of all....

The light showers down the pyramid, down and through your body....

It fills your stomach, your sexual organs, everything down to your feet....

Imagine the base of the pyramid connecting to the earth, deeply grounded in the earth, part of the earth....

It is a wonderful, powerful center of energy and consciousness. In this center, we are fully aware of our roots in the earth....

We are made of solid earth — we are miracle creations....

Breathe deeply for a while into the energy center of your root chakra, your deepest grounding into the earth....

Fill it with healing light....

Then imagine your energy rising up the pyramid, and filling your second chakra, your sexual center, with radiant healing light....

Your sexual center, the source of powerful creative energies....

Fill this center with healing light....

Let your fears dissolve in that light....
Breathe deeply for a while into the endless, expansive creativity of your second chakra....

Now feel your energy move up into your abdomen, your *hara*, your third chakra....
It is the center of your power....
Breathe healing light into this energy center....
All is well....
Rest in this center for a while....
Feel it relax and heal....
Feel it become filled with powerful creative energy....
The energy of life....
Breathe deeply for a while into the endless, expansive energy of your third chakra....

Now feel that light energy move into your heart....
Let everything lighten and expand....
Take a deep breath, and fill your chest with healing oxygen....
Feel your heart expand....
Love is the answer, love is the end of the journey....
Love is ultimate wisdom, for it awakens all the higher energy centers, and moves us into the higher levels of consciousness....

Love is the answer, love is the key.
It can open any door, give us eyes to see.
In our hearts lies a secret, and it sets us free —
all we need is love.

Breathe deeply for a while into the endless, expansive energy of your heart, your fourth chakra....

Now feel that loving energy move up into your throat....
Feel your throat being healed by every cool breath....
Feel the radiant life energy in your throat awakening your voice....
You are a unique creative genius, and you have much to say to the world....
Breathe deeply for a while into the endless, expansive creative energy of your fifth chakra....

Now feel that radiant energy move up into your third eye, right between and above your physical eyes....
See the endless fields of light that are within you....
Sit for a while, and see and feel the ocean of inner peace....

Now move your light energy up to the crown of your head....
Feel it vibrate and expand into the endless radiant spheres of the highest levels of consciousness....

**You are That.
You are one with all that is.**

This is your true nature. You are a being of light, and life, and love, an eternal part of an eternal shining creation of the forces of life.

We are the creation of the forces of life,

an eternal blend of ecstasy and strife,

living as long as the universe stays,

which is forever, through our galaxies' nights and days.

From the big bang's beginning

to the black hole's destruction

is but a day in the life of our cosmic construction.

We'll live forever, we're the stuff of stars,

ever growing, ever changing,

born into this life, born into that,

changing this form for the one that comes next,

an eternal part of an eternal creation,

a quintessential piece of divine revelation!

Maslow's Pyramid

In the West, the power of visualizing pyramids has been understood for a very long time as well, and just as in the East, there are many different versions. There are just two that I often reflect upon: Maslow's pyramid and the pyramid of growth, expansion, and wealth. Each one is a great source of wisdom — the kind of wisdom that can guide us often during the day, and help us make decisions that are completely aligned with our highest good.

Abraham Maslow was one of the founders of humanistic psychology. He is best known for his concept of the hierarchy of human needs, which I learned about in a college course and then over the years adapted (mostly subconsciously) to my own needs. It is a useful tool to help understand a complex world.

Maslow's original hierarchy of human needs is diagrammed as a pyramid with biological and physical needs at the bottom — the basic life needs of air, food, shelter. Above these are safety needs: protection and security. Above these are belongingness and love needs: family, affection, relationships, work group. Above these are esteem needs: achievement, status, responsibility. Finally, at the very top of the pyramid is the level of consciousness he called, quite strikingly, *self-actualization*: personal growth and fulfillment.

(Thank you, Wikipedia, for reminding me of Maslow's original concept — over the years I gradually changed it, put it in my own words, and made it simpler. Adapt any of this in any ways you wish.)

Our journey in life begins with having to meet the very basic needs of food and shelter; then we grow into fulfilling higher and higher needs. Along the way, we have what Maslow called *peak experiences* — glimpses of the wonder of what is — until finally we are able to fulfill our greatest potential and become *actualized.*

Why is this even included in a book of modern, practical magic? Because I've adapted the concept in a way that has helped me not only attain success personally but also understand the world's problems more clearly, so that I can actually do something that contributes to a better world by helping others move up the pyramid.

The people at the bottom of the pyramid need food and shelter, air and clean water. If we don't have these things in our lives, the need to get them dominates our consciousness. Once we get them, we rise up on the pyramid to the level of safety and security. Once these needs are fulfilled, we rise up to the level where physical healing or therapy may be necessary before we can continue further up the pyramid.

Once we have these basic needs met, we move up into the realms of education. Here, on these expansive, exciting levels of consciousness, we can learn what we need in life to move even further up the pyramid, up to the top, into peak experiences of self-actualization, self-realization, and fulfillment.

As we move up the pyramid, we find we naturally want to help others come along with us. There is a lot we can do, individually and in various groups. And there is a lot that needs to be done — and that is the Great Work ahead of us.

Every government should feed and house and protect and educate its people — those are obviously primary purposes of a government. Most governments fail to do this, however, so it's up to all of us to do something to help out. For most countries, it takes a creative series of partnerships with individuals, nonprofits, businesses, and governments to fulfill the basic needs of the people.

There is something you can do to help make the world a better place. There are an infinite number of possibilities for every one of us. You're probably doing something already, for if you're reading this, you're obviously on the higher levels of the pyramid of human consciousness — moving through higher education into self-actualization.

> Reflect on this:
> Our basic needs are simply here to be met so we can focus on and attain what is important in life.
> And what's important?
> That's up to you to decide....
> Reflect on this for a while....
>
> It includes remembering and treasuring those peak experiences we have all had....
> We have all had flashes of illumination....

**The human opportunity, the religions tell us,
is to transform our flashes of insight
into abiding light.**

— HUSTON SMITH

So be it. So it is!

The Pyramid of Growth, Expansion, and Wealth

Another powerful thing to imagine is that we contain within us a pyramid of growth, expansion, and wealth. Financial planners the world over use this image; it can be a very helpful thing to reflect upon occasionally.

Over the years, I have imagined, and sometimes written down, this kind of pyramid in different forms. I'll suggest one here, but it is a suggestion only. As with all of the other material in this course, take it and play with it and change it in whatever ways suit you.

Take a deep breath, and relax....
Imagine that within your expansive mind is a vast pyramid that symbolizes and contains your wealth, assets, and property....
Ask or pray for the guidance to manage your pyramid of wealth skillfully, so it is ever growing....
As in the words of the famous prayer of Jabez from the Bible, pray to enlarge your territory — and never hurt anyone in the process....

The base of your pyramid consists of the solid assets of your cash and investment portfolio, any real estate you may own, and any retirement plan you may have in place....
These are the solid blocks that build the foundation of your wealth....
Imagine they are invested so they provide a passive

income that continually adds to the foundation of your pyramid, so it grows and grows....

Above these are blocks containing other assets, such as art, jewelry, gold, musical instruments, collectibles....
Above these are more liquid cash you have to spend, donate, invest....
Visualize your liquid cash reserves to be growing steadily as well, expanding the body of the pyramid....

What's at the top? Imagine a shower of wealth and abundance in all forms....
It continually builds the pyramid below....
And it showers others in the world with your generosity and support....
Imagine you contain within yourself an ever-growing pyramid of growth, expansion, and wealth.

Find the image that works best for you. These types of visualizations provide powerful instructions to our limitless subconscious mind.

**You
are a unique
creative genius, capable
of realizing your most expansive
dreams in life and fulfilling your true purpose,
moving up, and helping others move up, the pyramid
of human consciousness to self-actualization and fulfillment.**

So be it. So it is!

6

TIME AND MONEY AND THE CORE BELIEF PROCESS

Mind is the master power that molds and makes,
And we are Mind, and evermore we take
The tool of Thought, and, shaping what we will,
Bring forth a thousand joys, a thousand ills.
We think in secret, and it comes to pass —
Our world is but our looking glass.

— JAMES ALLEN, *As You Think*

We saw that James Allen quote earlier (in chapter 2). It's worth rereading, and pondering — and sometimes it just might come to mind, unbidden, in the perfect moment.

The Root of the Problem

This chapter takes us to the root of the problems and obstacles we encounter on our magical path, our quest to create something out of nothing. We can do all the magic ritual and prayer and affirmation and visualization in the world, but if we don't change the underlying beliefs we may have that we're not capable — for any reason at all — of creating what we desire, then those limiting beliefs will undermine our dreams, plans, and actions.

To put it simply:

**Any magic we perform will not be effective
if we believe, underneath it all,
that we are incapable of creating our dreams.**

It all gets down to our underlying beliefs. It's definitely a good use of our time to take a good look at those beliefs. If we're not creating what we want in life, we have to become aware of the beliefs we have that are limiting us and holding us back from realizing our dreams. Becoming aware of our beliefs is the first step toward changing those beliefs. And when we change our beliefs, we change our life and our world.

Most of us, when we think about it, have a large set of underlying beliefs, and many of them contradict and even conflict with each other. We know we have strengths, talents, something unique to offer the world. We all have dreams and desires and passions. Yet most of us also believe it's really hard to succeed — so few people do it, after all. Life isn't easy; it's difficult; it's hard. It's a struggle to make ends meet. It's stressful!

In my late twenties, I learned something about our beliefs from a man named Ken Keyes Jr. that has made a huge difference in my life:

**Our beliefs are not true in themselves,
but they become true in our experience
if we believe them.**

We think it's the other way around, don't we? We believe what we believe because that's the way it is. But it turns out that's not true. We believe what we believe because we were told it was true, and we accepted it as true, and then, sure enough, it became true in our experience.

We developed a whole set of beliefs about ourselves and our world when we were young, some good, some bad, some beautiful, some ugly. Some of these beliefs have changed over time, some of them haven't, and a lot of them contradict each other. As long as these beliefs remain unexamined, they run our lives. Once we look at them clearly, we can begin to change them.

We can change all kinds of beliefs, including our deepest core beliefs about time and money — two essential ingredients of a life worth living. I've written about this before — some of the following is excerpted from *The Millionaire Course*, with new material added.

Understanding Time

Understanding time, and even mastering time, is not an impossible thing to do. It involves looking at our beliefs about time and being willing to change some of those old beliefs. There are many people who have different sets of beliefs about time, and so live in a completely different reality.

It's odd when you think about it: We all have a large, complex set of beliefs about time, yet we almost never think about those beliefs, and rarely — if ever — examine them consciously. When we do give them some thought, we soon realize that, like all our other beliefs, they are not necessarily true in themselves — but they are self-fulfilling if we believe them to be true.

Until I was thirty-five or so, I believed that there wasn't enough time — or money — in my life. The two were related somehow, and I struggled with both. For some reason, God didn't create enough. Time was always passing me by. There wasn't enough time to do what I wanted to do. Things would always take so much more time than I planned on. Time was flying.

Do any of these beliefs sound familiar?

Then something shifted in my belief system. I found I could make a conscious choice to change my beliefs to create more time in my life. I'm almost certain that the single most effective thing I did was to keep affirming these words with my goals: *in an easy and relaxed manner, in a healthy and positive way, in its own perfect time, for the highest good of all.*

I have all the time I need. I very rarely have to rush anywhere. I have plenty of free time, all the time for relaxation that I want and need, all the time I want for my creative work, and plenty of time for friends and family. My entire experience of reality has shifted as my belief that I have enough has become dominant over my earlier belief of scarcity.

Are you often stressed, running some kind of race with the clock? What are you thinking, what are you telling yourself at the time? Did the universe somehow not create enough time for you?

Take a good look at your beliefs about time, and take the necessary steps to change them.

> **Affirm your goals are being realized,**
> **in an easy and relaxed manner,**
> **a healthy and positive way,**
> **in their own perfect time,**
> **for the highest good of all.**
>
> **These words are true magic:**
> **They can help you master time and money.**

We are slaves to the clock only as long as we believe we are. We are perfectly capable of mastering time. Within these pages are the keys that show us how. We live in an abundant universe, and that includes an abundance of time, money, and everything else.

Mastering Time

There is a magical path, a short path, to easily and effortlessly creating more time in your life. Just ponder this, and see if you can get it and then apply it in your life: Our beliefs are not true in themselves, but they become true in our experience if we believe them. This is true of all our beliefs about time, so it's definitely worthwhile to look at them.

When you can change your beliefs about time, you can master time. You can have plenty of time — more than enough time.

How do you change your beliefs? Go through the Core Belief Process — it's coming up next. Or do something even simpler:

Take a moment, take a deep breath, and relax....
Now state out loud (or very clearly to yourself in your mind) the answer to this question: What do I believe about time?
Express your beliefs about time in the simplest words possible....
(An example: *There's not enough time to do what I want.*)
Then find an affirmation that directly contradicts and counteracts those beliefs — something like:

I have plenty of time to do what I want,
in an easy and relaxed manner,
a healthy and positive way.

You can make the conscious choice to stop programming yourself that there is not enough time, and start programming yourself that you have all the time in the world.

You can master time.

Believe that it's possible, and it will be possible for you. Believe that it's true, and it will be true for you in your life and in your world.

Understanding Money

Most of us have a mass of confused beliefs about money. Until I turned thirty-five, I certainly did. There wasn't enough money, ever. It was scarce, hard to come by. Money doesn't grow on trees, after all. I believed it took hard work, discipline, intelligence, talent, luck, perseverance to make money — things I didn't believe I had or didn't want to do. I believed it took money to make money — and since I didn't have any, the cards were stacked against me. The rich get richer and the poor get poorer. A fool and his money are soon parted — and I believed, deep down, when I looked at my history with money, I was definitely a fool.

It was certainly true in my experience. Whatever I made evaporated quickly. Besides, I even felt that maybe money really was the root of all evil. Money corrupts. The pursuit of the almighty dollar distracts us from what is important in life. It is impossible for a rich person to be a good person.

Do any of these beliefs sound familiar to you? What are you thinking, what are you telling yourself about money?

Do you believe there is a shortage of money? Did the universe somehow not create enough for you? Do you believe you don't have what it takes to make a substantial amount of money? Do you believe money is hard to get? Do you believe that if you get it, someone else will have to do without it, or in some other way be hurt by it? Do you believe money will corrupt you? Or distract you from the important things in life?

Take a good look at your beliefs about money, and take the necessary steps to change them. Do the Core Belief Process that follows, as many times as necessary. After I went through the process — several times, over several years — something shifted in my belief system about money and its availability. I came to see and believe that money could be a tremendous force for good in my life, and in the lives of many others. I came to avoid so many potential problems with money by constantly reminding myself that every step I was taking was for the highest good of all.

**You can make a conscious decision
to change your beliefs
and create more money in your life.
The choice is up to you.**

I'm almost certain that the single most effective thing I did in this arena was simply to ask — and to pray — for a specific amount of money, one that was an expansive leap for me to even imagine.

As soon as you ask for an expansive amount of money, you begin to get creative new ideas, and different possibilities come to mind that could very well result in the kind of money you're asking for. Different opportunities suddenly appear — and it usually feels as though those opportunities had been right in front of you all along, but you just hadn't seen them before.

Some of these ideas and opportunities lead me to paths I don't want to take or have no interest in or energy for; some lead to prospects I reject because they don't feel easy, relaxed, healthy, or positive in some way. But some of the possibilities excite something in me, and take me in new directions that are challenging and fulfilling.

I live in a world that is truly abundant, and the universe provides amply for me. I have discovered ways to create income streams from a variety of sources. I have received what I have asked for, no more, no less. This is certainly a vital key:

**You will receive what you ask for,
no more, no less.**

My entire experience of reality has shifted as newer beliefs gradually replaced my earlier beliefs of scarcity. I don't work for money anymore; I do what I love, and there is always plenty of money. This is what I believe, and this is what has come true in my life.

Mastering Money

Our beliefs are not true in themselves, but they become true in our experience if we believe them. This is true of all our beliefs about money, so it's definitely worthwhile to look at them.

When you can change your beliefs about money, you can master money. You can have plenty of money — more than enough money. How do you change your beliefs? Go through the Core Belief Process that follows. Or make it even simpler and just do this brief little exercise:

Take a moment, take a deep breath, and relax, from head to toe....
Now state out loud (or very clearly to yourself in your mind) the answer to this question: What do I believe about money?

Express your beliefs about money in the simplest
words possible....
(An example: *There's not enough money to do what I
want. I'm not capable of making enough money.*)
Then find affirmations that directly contradict and
counteract those beliefs — something like:

**I am sensible and in control of my finances;
I am creating total financial success,
in an easy and relaxed manner,
a healthy and positive way.**

You can make the conscious choice to stop programming
yourself that there is not enough money, and start programming yourself that you have all the money in the world.

You can be a master of money.

Mastering money is not all that difficult. Believe that it's possible, and it will be possible for you. Believe that it's true, and
it will be true for you in your life and in your world. If you
have trouble believing it, go through the following process
with an open mind, and see what happens.

The Core Belief Process

Fortunately for all of us, there is a simple process we can use
to consciously change our beliefs about time, money, or anything else — any beliefs that are undermining our dreams

of magically creating a better life and a better world. I've included it in other books, and I have to include it here. It's worth repeating until your life and your world change for the better. (It took me about seven years, going through it many times, before the process finally had a direct, powerful, lasting effect on my life.)

You can do this process at any time, but the best times are when you're upset about something, when you're struggling with a *problem*. All it requires is answering these questions as honestly as you can, either in your head or on paper:

1. *What is the problem?* Just describe the situation, for a minute or two.

2. *What emotions are you feeling?* Just name them, in a word or two. Is there fear, frustration, anger, guilt, sadness? Sometimes just the act of naming the emotions will be enough for you to let at least some of them go. Other times, you have to go through all the steps of the process before your emotions shift.

3. *What physical sensations are you feeling?* Take a minute to tune in to your body. Briefly describe what you feel happening physically.

4. *What are you thinking about?* Take a few minutes and say out loud or write down what has been going through your mind. Is there a repetitive stream of thoughts you've been having lately? What are those recurrent thoughts?

5. *What is the worst thing that could happen in this situation?* What is the worst-case scenario that you can imagine? If that happened, what would be the very worst thing that could happen to you? It's good to shed some light on your deepest fears, because you come to realize that the chances of those deep fears actually being realized are very slim indeed.

6. *What is the best thing that could happen?* What would you like to have happen, ideally? What is your ideal scene for this area of your life?

7. *What fear or limiting belief is keeping you from creating what you want?* Now we're getting to the core of the problem: What fear or limiting belief can you identify that's preventing you from creating your ideal scene in this particular situation? State it as simply as you can — the simpler, the better. *I'm a fool with money....I don't have what it takes....It's so hard to succeed....It's all so stressful and unhealthy....*

8. *What affirmation can you come up with that contradicts and counteracts that negative or limiting belief?* Put it in directly opposite words, if you can. Play with it until you find an affirmation that feels good to you and speaks to you in your own unique way. *I am sensible and in control of my finances....I am creating total financial success....I am now creating abundance in my life....I am living the life of my*

dreams, in an easy and relaxed manner, in a healthy and positive way.

9. *Say or write your affirmation repeatedly over the next days, weeks, and months.* Write it down, and put it in places where you see it often. Repeat it — or repeat them, if you have several — in the mornings and throughout the day whenever you remember, especially when doubts and fears arise, as they almost surely will. When you repeat it enough, it will eventually become more powerful than your doubts and fears.

Then the magic of creation happens, in an easy and relaxed manner, a healthy and positive way, in its own perfect time, for the highest good of all.

When I went through this simple process, startling changes started to happen almost immediately (although, as I said, it took me about seven years before the process had a lasting impact and my life changed dramatically). I didn't have to believe the process worked, because I saw it working in my life.

The secret of this simple yet powerful form of magic is given very clearly in the Bible:

> **And you shall decree a thing,**
> **and it will be given unto you.**
> **And light will shine upon your ways.**
>
> — JOB 22:28

167

We have heard so many of these things over and over. Now these ancient truths are beginning to be realized in the lives of a great many people. Once we see the power we have to affect our own beliefs, we see that we can change our lives — and change the world as well.

We see, in fact, that we have everything we need in this moment to realize our greatest dreams. We find that we have within us the ability to dream a lofty dream, affirm that it is coming true, and take the steps necessary to realize it.

These are the keys to the direct path — the path of real, effective magic.

**You have everything you need
in this moment
to realize your greatest dreams.**

So be it. So it is!

7

PRAYER AND MANTRA THROUGHOUT THE DAY

*What we are today comes from our thoughts of yesterday,
and our present thoughts build our life tomorrow;
our life is the creation of our mind.*

— BUDDHA in the Dhammapada
(and JAMES ALLEN)

We have only this moment, now. The past is but a figment of our imagination; the future does not exist. Life is now. (Thank you, Eckhart Tolle, and the Dalai Lama, for reminding us of that so beautifully.)

In this moment, now, we can think only one thought at a time. That thought has creative power, for good or for ill. The more we consciously choose good thoughts in the moment, the more our lives are filled with good. Every thought we have programs our subconscious mind. Every thought has results.

So it's certainly good to do whatever we can do throughout the day to remind ourselves to program our subconscious with powerful, creative thoughts. There are hundreds and hundreds — *thousands* — of possibilities. I suggest a great many throughout this book. Take them and change them and make them your own.

> Prayer is the contact of your mind
> with God-Mind,
> in a way that shall result
> in bringing to pass a desired good.
>
> — ERNEST HOLMES

> The best prayers
> are short prayers.
>
> — MARTIN LUTHER

Morning Meditation and Prayer

Every moment is a magical creation, but there is an especially brilliant, creative energy in the morning. It's an ideal time for meditation or prayer. Your morning prayer can take many different forms. Use these words as a suggestion only, to help you create your own ritual and prayer.

When we first awaken in the morning, there is a moment when we are still connected to dream worlds, and even a moment when part of us still lingers in that soundless, wordless space of deep sleep. Try to be as aware as possible of your state of being as soon as you wake up. You still have a connection to something vast, far beyond your body.

Lie back for a moment, and relax and recall the deep relaxation you feel physically. Remember and enjoy the deep pleasure of dreamless sleep.

Then recall any dreams you can. Remember the trick (mentioned in chapter 3) called "grasping the tail of the snake" — try to remember the last image of your dream, and work backward, recalling as much as possible. Dreams are powerful, as we all know: They are essential therapy, and so much more as well. Our dreams bring us messages from our vast subconscious mind.

> **Some of the messages in our dreams**
> **are so powerful that they can guide us**
> **every moment of our waking lives.**

This is true for both kinds of dreams we have: the dreams we have when sleeping and the dreams we dare to imagine when we're awake.

Once you've relaxed and remembered your dreams, get up as quietly as possible and go to your favorite place for your morning prayer. It can be outside or inside. It's best when it's private and quiet, though it can be done anywhere. (I've done versions of it walking down noisy, busy streets in New York and LA.)

Take a deep breath, and relax as you exhale....
Take a deep breath, and as you exhale, let all thoughts go....
Simply be quiet, in the moment....
Feel the energy of the morning....
Hear the sounds....
See *what is*....
Take a moment to be quiet, peaceful, still....

Whether in a city, in the country, or in between, you are surrounded by the wonders of creation....
Take a moment to address the being or the force that has created the miracles that are all around you....
Summon that being or force to you with your thoughts, or with whispered or spoken words....
Give it/him/her a name. Many call it God; use that if it feels right. Or call it Creator, or Great Spirit, or Great Mystery, or any other name you choose....
For now, we call it Creator....

Summon the Creator to you....
Start with thanks, with gratitude for *what is*....
Give thanks for the miraculous creation that you are a vital part of....
Thank the Creator for something specific in your life; find something new every day....
You've added something to your gratitude list, and you realize the list of things you are grateful for is endless....

Now ask to be guided by the forces of creation throughout the day....

Ask for any particular guidance the Creator has for you this moment....
Be silent, and listen within for whatever words come along....
Let the stillness speak to you....

Ask and you shall receive.

Ask the highest, most powerful forces of creation for guidance, and you will receive it.

So be it. So it is.

Now turn toward the sun. Even if it is hidden from our view, blocked by the earth or by clouds, the sun is always there, always shining, and it has been shining for billions of years, showering the earth with light, filling the earth with life.

Find the sun, and face that direction.

Face the sun, and let it fill your body with its light....
Feel the sun's radiance at the top of your head....
Feel it move down your spine....
You are a pillar of light....
This is *what is*.

You are made of the stuff of stars....
You are one with the source of creation....
One with the Creator....
You are filled with light and healing life energy....

That energy within you is radiant, completely pure....
It is the essence of who you are, and will continue for-
ever and ever....
You are life itself, in all its power and glory....

Make sure to do some kind of prayer every morning. If you're
in a hurry, you can do it in a very short time — under a minute if necessary. But do something. Make it a habit. Even if
you think you have no time at all, take a deep breath, and say
something like this:

> **Thank you for the light and life within me.**
> **Guide me throughout the day.**

We all know and sense that the morning is an extraordinary
time. The night is turning into day; the light is returning into
our lives. Take the energy of that sun and imagine it pouring
through your whole body, blessing and healing every cell of
your body, nurturing every cell.

In that moment, you are acknowledging the wonder of what
is. All life is a miracle. All life is a magical creation. The life
and light within you are working miracles in your life, every
moment of every day. Affirm something like this:

> **Every day, in every way,**
> **the light and life within me**
> **are working miracles in my life**
> **and in the world.**

In the silence of our morning mind, the words and images we bring to mind can remain with us throughout the day, and lighten our lives.

IN THE SILENCE OF OUR MORNING MIND

We awaken from our sleep....
The last image of a dream remains,
and we remember something magical....

The world outside wakes up too....
And we listen, without a thought....
Hear the wind singing its song....
See the trees swaying in their gentle dance....
And we know, we realize:
I am that!
I am that wind, and those trees....
And the whole precious world in its dance of creation.

Remembering Throughout the Day

Find some way or other to keep reminding yourself of your prayers or affirmations or mantras or other phrases of magic or inspiration throughout the day. After all:

Your thoughts and words have creative power.
Watch what you think and say
every moment of the day.

People wince when I say this. They're thinking, *Oh no! Do I have to be aware of every thought, every word?* Most people go through most of the day being completely oblivious to most of their thoughts.

There is good news, however, even for the most desperately lost and confused: The positive thoughts that we consciously repeat are far more powerful than the negative ones, and we only need to keep thinking those positive thoughts a small percentage of the time for them to have a huge impact in our lives.

The flight path of our lives of magical creation is exactly the same as the flight path of an airplane, in at least one powerful way: A plane is off course over 95 percent of the time, but the pilot keeps correcting and correcting, and the plane arrives at its destination.

As soon as we decide to become the magicians and creative geniuses we are all capable of being, we realize that the tools, the vehicles, we need are waiting at our disposal. When we make any kind of plan to achieve our goals and dreams, we set our course. Fortunately, we can be off course most of the time, but as long as we keep returning to the words that inspire us and empower us, as long as we keep returning to our goals and dreams, we're back on course, and we will arrive at the destination we've chosen.

**We can be off course most of the time
and still reach our destination.
All it takes is a bit of ongoing course correction.**

Reciting Poems

This powerful practice is fun as well: Find a poem you love — something you enjoy reading — and memorize it and repeat it during the day. Don't underestimate the power of this fun little thing to do!

For years, the poem that is the first page, the frontispiece, in *As You Think* — the poem that opened the previous chapter of this book — was a mainstay in my life. I memorized it and repeated it until its words had permeated my subconscious. Here it is, once again:

> **Mind is the master power that molds and makes,**
> **And we are Mind, and evermore we take**
> **The tool of Thought, and, shaping what we will,**
> **Bring forth a thousand joys, a thousand ills.**
> **We think in secret, and it comes to pass —**
> **Our world is but our looking glass.**

After several years of repeating that poem, I started repeating the second poem in the book as well, where James Allen quoted a poem by Ella Wheeler Wilcox. These poems can have a deep effect on every day of your life if you memorize them and say or think them repeatedly for a few days or weeks:

> **You will be what you will to be;**
> **Let failure find its false content**
> **In that poor word "environment,"**
> **But Spirit scorns it, and is free.**

It masters time, it conquers space,
It cows that boastful trickster Chance,
And bids the tyrant Circumstance
Uncrown, and fill a servant's place.

The human Will, that force unseen,
The offspring of a deathless Soul,
Can hew a way to any goal,
Though walls of granite intervene.

Be not impatient in delay,
But wait as one who understands;
When spirit rises and commands,
The gods are ready to obey.

When your spirit rises and commands, you summon the creative forces of the universe to assist you. We'll come back to this poem later, because the repetition of these words is a powerful magical ritual in itself, a summoning of creative forces.

Poetry, prayer, mantras, affirmations, songs, jingles, rhymes — no matter what form they take, when powerful words are imprinted in your phenomenal mind, there are miraculous results.

Reciting Phrases

It's true as well for short phrases and declarations. When you memorize and recite them, you summon the creative energies that are in those words.

Just a few phrases repeated many times over many months have deeply affected my life. Here are the four most powerful phrases I've found so far, in the order I discovered them. I put them on my wall in big letters and repeated them hundreds of times.

> You will become as great
> as your dominant aspiration....
> If you cherish a vision, a lofty ideal in your heart,
> you will realize it.
>
> — JAMES ALLEN, *As You Think*

> Within every adversity is the seed
> of an equal or greater benefit.
> Within every problem is an opportunity.
> Even in the knocks of life
> we can find great gifts.
>
> — Inspired by NAPOLEON HILL and
> the Bhagavad Gita

> To offer no resistance to life
> is to be in a state of grace, ease, and lightness.
>
> — ECKHART TOLLE, *The Power of Now*

> The happiness that is derived from some secondary source
> is never very deep.
> It is only a pale reflection of the joy of Being,
> the vibrant peace that you find within
> as you enter the state of nonresistance.
>
> — ECKHART TOLLE, *The Power of Now*

Find the phrases that move you deeply and repeat them until they are deeply imprinted in your subconscious mind. Those words have the power to fill you with energy, light, and life.

A Ring of Power

Pick a ring, any ring you choose, to remind you that you already are a creative magician, able to create what you wish out of nothing at all.

Wear the ring wherever it feels good. (I like it on my dominant, active side — right, if you're right-handed, left if you're left-handed.) When you extend your arm to the heavens, when you do anything at all throughout the day, let your ring become a reminder of the power of creation that flows through your whole being, every moment, beginning with the highest levels of spirit and moving down into concrete, solid form.

Let your ring remind you that you have the tools you need in your magician's toolkit.

> **You know enough already.**
> **You have all the answers within.**
> **You simply need to inquire within.**

If in doubt, just keep repeating this great affirmation: *I am enough! I am enough!* You're affirming what is true, and your ring will remind you, every day: You have everything you need; all the answers you need are already within you.

**I have everything I need
to enjoy the here and now.**

O HEALING WATER MEDITATION

Sometimes the most powerful meditations are the shortest
and simplest. This one only requires a glass of water and a few
seconds of time.

> Pour a glass of clear, clean water. Drink it slowly....
> Feel it going down your throat, cooling and cleansing
> and healing....
> Say something like this:*

O Healing Water, O Healing Water
I've come to join you today
To wash my sorrows, my cares and pain,
To wash all illness away

O Healing Water
You bring life and light
To every cell of my body
And you remind me, always,
I am life, and light, and love.

---

* "O Healing Water" is a beautiful song written by Summer Raven, recorded
with the lyrics on my album *Seeds* and recorded as an instrumental (without the lyrics) on *Solo Flight*. I have changed and added words in this little
meditation.

ELIXIR OF THE GODS MEDITATION

You can do a similar meditation with fruit juice as well, of course. Pick your favorite juice, or come up with some tasty blend of different juices. Or have a smoothie!

> Pour a glass of fruit juice....
> Hold it to the heavens....
> It is an elixir of the gods....
>
> Sip it slowly....
> Feel it going down your throat, cleansing, healing....
> Feel it fill you with vibrant energy....
>
> O powerful elixir!
> You bring life and light
> To every cell of my body
> And you remind me, always,
> I am life, and light, and love.

SPIRIT MEDITATION

We'll end this chapter with two more meditations and one more prayer. The first is a meditation that summons spirit, and fills us with spirit, very much like the Middle Pillar Meditation. It's short and simple and easy to recall throughout the day.

> Relax....
> Take a deep, cleansing breath, and relax your body....
> Take another deep breath, and relax your mind, let all thought go....
> Take another breath, and let everything go....

Feel your presence within....
Feel that you are floating in an ocean of grace, ease, and lightness....
Feel the energy of life itself permeating every cell of your body....

Now feel the energy at the very top of your head....
Imagine your crown chakra is open and radiant....
Its radiant light fills you, opening up your sixth chakra as well — your visionary third eye....
There is a presence there, a being of light and love....
It is your spirit, your highest self, your eternal being....
Imagine that spirit merging with your physical body, infusing every cell with its healing life energy....
You are filled with light....
You are spirit....

Ask your spirit any question you may have, and listen for an answer....
Ask spirit to be with you, every moment of the day....

Affirm and remember:

I am filled with spirit,
every moment.

So be it. So it is!

SPIRIT MAGICIAN MEDITATION

When we go on these guided meditations, these journeys of pure imagination, we remember what we experience just as clearly as we remember things that happen in the so-called real world. In our inner journeys, we go places and create sanctuaries and meet Guides. We remember their words; they are perfect for us. And we find we can summon the healing and creative energies of their presence into our daily lives.

It all starts in our imagination — when you become a magician in your imagination, you suddenly find yourself doing magic in the real world. We've already met our Inner Guides. They are allies that support us every step of the way. They answer any questions and give us the inner guidance we need.

The Magician within is a bit different from your Inner Guide — at least the way I see it. Your Inner Guide comes to you from a distance, and has a presence and personality that feels different from your own. The Magician is *you* — the highest part of you, pure spirit. When you imagine the Inner Magician, you're summoning the highest, most evolved parts of yourself.

The Magician points upward to the heavens with his or her right hand, and downward to earth with the left — signifying the Magician is able to create by beginning in the highest spiritual and mental spheres, and then bringing these energies down into physical form, grounded in the earth.

**When you imagine the Magician within you,
you summon the creative force of the universe
to do what you will.**

Relax....
Take a deep, cleansing breath, and relax your body....

Take another deep breath, and relax your mind, let all
thought go....
Take another breath, and let *everything go*....
Bathe in the light of your being....
Feel that you're floating in an ocean of light, with
grace, ease, and lightness....
Feel the healing life energy that permeates every cell of
your body....

Feel the warmth at the crown of your head....
There is a radiant light there....
A golden glowing crown of light....
It touches you, it is part of you, and it extends through-
out your body and throughout the whole universe....

There is a presence emerging out of the field of spirit,
a being of light and love....
It is your spirit, your highest self, your eternal being....
It takes the shape of the Magician that you are....
The Magician points their right hand high upward....
Stretching the arm tall....
In doing so, they summon the creative energies of the
universe....
The Magician points the left hand downward, taking
the highest energies of the heavens and bringing them
down to earth....
And the formless becomes form....

Be with your Magician in silence for a bit....
Let your Inner Magician guide you to do any rituals or
say any prayers or affirmations....

Ask any questions you have, and listen for the answers....

Ask that the Magician guide you and empower you every step of your magical journey....

Imagine the presence, the spirit, of the Magician merging with your physical body, infusing every cell with the power of its life energy....

You are filled with light. You are spirit....

You are a Magician.

So be it. So it is.

THE ETERNAL PRAYER

Say this prayer while sitting quietly. Visualize it, in whatever way you can, as you say it.

> **I close my eyes and see a field of light,**
> **and I feel that light and life**
> **in every cell of my body,**
> **nurturing and healing every cell.**
> **And I know that light, and life, and love,**
> **is who and what I am,**
> **now and forever.**

Amen.

Sit with a loved one, or just imagine a loved one, and say the prayer together. It's a wonderful prayer to say with children as well, especially when it's time to sleep.

We close our eyes and see a field of light,
and we feel that light and life
in every cell of our bodies,
nurturing and healing every cell.
And we know that light, and life, and love,
is who and what we are,
now and forever.

Amen!

MAGICAL RELATIONSHIPS

The human opportunity, the religions tell us,
is to transform our flashes of insight
into abiding light.

— HUSTON SMITH

We've seen these words of Huston Smith earlier (in chapter 5) — it's one of my favorite quotes, up in big letters on the wall in front of my face as I write these words.

Those great words sum up what he learned from studying Buddhism and other religions for many years. Buddhist teachers often remind us that being born as a human being is a great and wonderful opportunity. This life we've been given, this moment, is an opportunity to remember our flashes of illumination, and turn those fleeting memories into lasting inner peace and abiding light. Our peak experiences can lead us to grow into the fullness of who we really are.

We all have this great opportunity — it's intrinsic to our human body, mind, and spirit. Once you see the opportunity you realize you have the ability to take advantage of it. We have all had flashes of illumination. We have all had moments of enlightenment, when we glimpse the wonder of what is.

We have the opportunity in this moment to focus on those flashes of illumination, and remember them. On a physical level, we can recall the feelings of those experiences in every cell of our bodies. And on some deep subconscious level, those recollections can affect us so deeply that they instill every moment of our lives with awareness and light.

Remember this when you're alone, and remember it when you're interacting with others. In the peak experiences you've had, you've realized the truth of *what is*.

In your flashes of illumination,
you realize the wonder
of who you really are.

This is a simple, powerful practice. It can transform us, and it can transform every relationship we have.

One way to look at the essence of magic is this: The magical approach involves finding the simple key — the brief, powerful, effective thing to do — that resolves problems quickly and makes life far more enjoyable, immediately, in this moment.

The magical path is one of the simplest paths of all. Much of it involves just finding the right phrases to repeat to ourselves. It's as simple as that. Don't deny its power because of its simplicity. An affirmation, a mantra, a prayer programs your limitless subconscious mind. It can affect every area of your life, including every relationship you have.

Our minds enjoy making things complex. In our intimate and work relationships, for example, we could do a lengthy study of how to improve ourselves. We could read piles of books, take all kinds of courses (many that conflict and disagree with each other), and spend hours on the Internet searching for solutions to our relationship problems at home and at work. It can all be very helpful, but it's also time-consuming.

The magical approach takes a lot less time. To use the words of Ella Wheeler Wilcox, *It masters time, it conquers space, it cows that boastful trickster Chance, and bids the tyrant Circumstance uncrown, and fill a servant's place.*

The magical path can be a powerful short path to creating the life of your dreams.

It's All about Relationships

We are constantly in relationship with each other, whether we happen to physically be near each other or not. We are constantly in relationship with nature and with our spirit as well. We are in relationship with the whole of the cosmos, the vast quantum field, simply because we are part of it. We are not isolated beings; we live in constant interplay with everything in the world around us.

> **Underneath the level of physical appearances**
> **and separate forms,**
> **you are one with all that is.**
>
> — ECKHART TOLLE, *The Power of Now*

Everything created in the entire universe involves a vast number of partnerships. Whether it's the simple elements combining when they're blown out of an exploding star, or the trillions of cells in our bodies working together in perfect harmony, or an artist or entrepreneur getting their work out into the world, successfully creating something is all about healthy, functioning relationships.

The simple, effective magical key to good relationships is something you've undoubtedly heard many times, so often it's almost become a cliché — but you've heard it so many times because it is so clear and powerful: The key is to create *win-win partnerships*.

> **Make every relationship a win-win partnership,**
> **with respect for everyone.**
> **This is a magical key to success in the world**
> **and to a fulfilling life as well.**

How do we do this? It's a great challenge for all of us. In this course, with the tools in this book, we can magically create successful relationships the same way we magically create anything else: We first do it in our inner world of imagination. We get the inside right, and the outside takes care of itself.

We start by just visualizing what we want — imagining it as clearly as possible. We keep focusing on it, and affirm it into being through the power of our focused thoughts and words.

> **We use one of the simplest forms**
> **of magic there is:**
> **We affirm it into being**
> **by the power of the spoken word.**

When you find the right affirmation, it can make every relationship in your life absolutely perfect.

Riane Eisler wrote a tremendous book called *The Power of Partnership*. She gives us a lens, as she calls it, to look at all of the essential relationships in our lives, and asks us to see whether there is partnership, based on respect, in our relationships or whether there is any kind of domination and exploitation, based on fear and a need to control in that relationship.

The great challenge for all of us is to create win-win partnerships in each of these areas. Let's go through each one, and see how we can have wonderful relationships — simply, easily, with sheer magic.

The first area Riane Eisler asks us to look at is brilliant and innovative, in my opinion:

Your Relationship with Yourself

Ask yourself: What is your relationship with yourself? Is it a good, fun, supportive relationship, or do you have an inner critic or critical parent beating you up, undermining your dreams? What is your self-image? Are you a healthy, creative dreamer and magician, or are there parts of you that are sabotaging you?

We all have inner critics, and they serve a valuable function. They provide us with an essential form of wisdom and guidance. But they can get out of line and be overbearing. We need to state our truth to them clearly, and find out how to work with them in creative ways that support our dreams and goals. Your inner critic can become a great ally, not an enemy. But that critic has to be dealt with firmly; it can't be allowed to banish and destroy the dreamer and visionary and magician that you also have within you.

Imagine that you are able by the power of your creative thought to bring your inner critics and inner parents to the negotiation table, and get them on your team so they're fully supportive of your dreams and plans. They can be powerful allies: They have insightful guidance on what steps to take and what steps to avoid taking.

Affirm something like this (find your own words):

I am enough.
I have everything I need
to enjoy my here and now.

> **Every day, in every way,**
> **I'm getting better and better.**

We need to be as gentle and accepting of ourselves as we want to be with our children, lovers, and best friends. We want to encourage our children and friends to be all that they can be, don't we? We want them to be happy, healthy, fulfilled. Give yourself the same kind of unwavering encouragement.

Tell yourself repeatedly and forcefully: You can do it! You can magically create the life of your dreams. It's not all that complicated or complex. It all begins within you, in your dreams, in your imagination. Remember the way Eckhart Tolle summed it all up in *The Power of Now*:

> **If you get the inside right,**
> **the outside will fall into place.**

So be it. So it is.

Can it really be that simple? Absolutely.

A magical key to a perfect relationship with yourself (and with anyone and everything else) was given by William Whitecloud in his book *The Magician's Way*:

> **Your focus creates your reality.**

That brilliantly sums up it: Your focus creates your reality, so focus on being a successful, capable, powerful person who has wonderful relationships with everyone along the way.

Affirm something like:

I am a visionary, a magician;
I am now creating the life of my dreams,
in an easy and relaxed manner,
a healthy and positive way,
in its own perfect time,
for the highest good of all.

Don't underestimate the power of these affirmations. If those words don't work for you, find words that do.

Intimate and Family Relationships

It all boils down to something very simple, doesn't it? *Your focus creates your reality, so get the inside right and focus on it, and the outside will take care of itself.* This is true in every kind of relationship we have, including intimate and family relationships.

How do we get the inside right? One way to do it is by the simple magical practice of visualizing — imagining — a wonderful partnership with those we love, where we support each other completely and love each other deeply, every moment of our lives.

Keep visualizing, keep imagining, keep focusing on your perfect intimate relationship. Let go of the doubts, worries, fears. Stop giving them your energy. Focus instead on what you really want in life. *Your focus creates your reality.* Affirm it is now manifesting in your life. Affirm something like:

My marriage and family life
are filled with grace, ease, and lightness.

I know some inner critics might be saying, *Is that all there is? We just mumble this little phrase over and over, and it's supposed to change our messed-up relationships? Hah!*

Don't be led off course by a misdirected inner critic. Don't let your fears and doubts overwhelm you. Just keep mumbling a few of these little phrases over and over for a while, and see what happens. It might be some tiny coincidence that helps you along, or it might be a full-blown magical miracle that plops directly into your life and changes everything.

Don't be misled by the simplicity of these tools: They have proven, over and over, to work. They give us a short path to success and even self-realization. We realize the wonder of what is.

Take a good, honest look at your intimate and family relationships. Are they stressful? Pleasurable? Generally happy and fulfilling? Is there a smooth, win-win partnership at work, or is there any kind of domination and exploitation going on?

Is there a need to control others? Or is there respect for everyone? That's the basic key to successful relationships: *respect*. Does everyone have a voice? Is love acknowledged in some ways?

Years ago, I wrote these words and printed them out in big letters and pasted them in a prominent place in our home:

What is the Purpose of a Family?

**To protect and support each one of us,
To be in partnership together,**

> To respect and love and listen to each other,
> To encourage each other to be happy and healthy,
> And to help us all fulfill our highest dreams.

So be it. So it is.

Your focus creates your reality, so focus on creating loving, supportive partnerships with everyone in your family. Find an affirmation that has the same power and effect on you as this one had on me:

> My marriage and family life are filled
> with grace, ease, and lightness.
>
> So be it. So it is.

Work Relationships

A great key to magically creating wonderful work relationships was given in one of the miracle stories in chapter 2. At the start of her career — and all through her wonderful thirty-year career — a woman kept affirming:

> I do wonderful work
> in a wonderful way
> with wonderful people
> for wonderful pay.

Those words triggered and empowered something deep in her subconscious mind. She had an inspiration to start her own business, collecting and selling things she loved — and she ended up doing wonderful work, in a wonderful way, with wonderful people, for wonderful pay.

I like the word *wonderful* — it has wonders in it; it has magic in it. You might prefer some other word or words, of course. Find what works for you.

As with every other type of relationship in our lives, the key to a wonderful workplace is to create win-win partnerships. You're all on the same team. You all have the same goals. Your workplace is where goals and dreams are realized.

Here's one way to express this magical key:

> **Your focus creates your reality.**
> **Focus on creating enjoyable win-win**
> **relationships in your work.**

Affirm and repeat something like (find appropriate words):

> **I work with wonderful people,**
> **in a wonderful way,**
> **I do what I love**
> **with grace, ease, and lightness.**
> **Every day in every way,**
> **we are getting better and better.**

Another way to express this great key is something we've all heard, many times before, something that can help us magically achieve our goals and dreams easily and effortlessly. There is a very good reason it's called the Golden Rule:

**Do unto others
as you would have them
do unto you.**

What do you want from the people you work with? You want respect. You want them to support you in reaching your dreams. You want success, as you choose to define it. You want a good share of the profits. You want to help others. You want to do something to make the world a better place.

**When you help others realize their dreams,
you are supported in realizing your dreams as well.**

If you're an employer, treat your employees just as you want to be treated. Respect them. Encourage them to dream, and help them fulfill their dreams. Let them share in the success of your company. Give them a good share of the profits (and they'll help you create far greater profits). Help them do something to make the world a better place.

In whatever work situation you have, the magical key is to work in partnership with everyone you interact with during the day — employees, customers, suppliers, service people. Real, lasting success is built on a firm foundation of ongoing win-win partnerships.

Any kind of domination or exploitation in any form inevitably creates more problems than it solves. The whole world has been given a great leader and teacher — a guiding light — who certainly knew this great key and expressed it with exquisite simplicity:

> **Love one another,**
> **as I have loved you.**
>
> — JESUS

This is the key to lasting success and a life of grace, ease, and lightness.

Community Relationships

Do we work in partnership with those in our neighborhoods and communities? How do we find the creative solutions that respect the people and the environment of the community? Is everyone respected, does everyone have a voice? How can our companies better support the communities they're located in?

More and more creative partnerships are being developed on a community level that address common problems. Working in partnership is the obvious key to resolving those problems.

Here's one way to express this key:

> **Your focus creates your reality.**
> **Focus on creating peaceful, fulfilling**
> **partnerships with those in your community.**

Affirm and repeat something like (find appropriate words):

> I am an asset to my community,
> working for the highest good of all
> with grace, ease, and lightness.

So be it. So it is.

Our National Community

Do we do our best to create smooth working partnerships with all of those who share our great country? Do we have a good working partnership with our government? In some ways, our government — founded by visionaries — has been a visionary partner, and in other ways, our government continues to act as an exploiter and dominator. Where is the system of domination still in place, and where is partnership operating? How can we move from the current system to one of greater partnership with everyone involved?

We have endless challenges ahead of us — and that means endless opportunities, benefits, and gifts *for all of us*. We're one big national family. We're a dysfunctional family, in too many ways — and the simple, magical key to overcome this is to accept as gracefully as possible all the inevitable differences that are between us and realize we need to work in partnership in spite of our differences.

We need to creatively work together in fulfilling our dreams and goals, and that means supporting others in reaching their goals. There will always be different points of view, left and right, conservative and liberal, so the challenging question for all of us is *How can we work together in partnership to reach our common goals — and even reach our very different goals?*

When we take a broad viewpoint, we can see that we all have goals and dreams that are similar. We all want respect. We all want life, liberty, and the pursuit of happiness — that's self-evident. So the way to resolve so many problems, whether they're personal, local, national, or international, is to sit down with people and ask how you can help each other.

How can I help you? How can you help me? How can we help each other fulfill our greatest dreams? That's a good question for us all to ask. When we're able to answer it, we're able to live together in peaceful, productive harmony.

Here's one way to express this key:

> **Your focus creates your reality.**
> **Focus on living freely and bravely,**
> **supporting life, liberty, and the pursuit of happiness**
> **and fulfillment for everyone in the country,**
> **everyone in the world.**

Affirm and repeat something like this (find appropriate words):

> **I live freely in a land of the free.**
> **My work and my life support everyone's**
> **life, liberty, and pursuit of happiness**
> **and fulfillment.**

So be it. So it is!

Our International Community

We're not only a national family, working together as a unit to build a great country. We're also an international family sharing a small planet. We've got to realize this: We're stuck with each other, and we're all one big dysfunctional family, so the best thing to do is learn how to live with each other without killing each other — the best thing to do is love and respect each other. Every one of us has a right to be here, and we all have a right to express our own points of view.

How successful are our partnerships with all the other governments and citizens of the world? Where is our country a partner and where is it still a dominator in the world arena? What can we do to bring our nation's actions closer to partnership with other nations? What can we persuade our government to do? What can we help our global companies to do? How can we work in partnership with our government and with our large global corporations? What can we do personally to live in greater partnership with the peoples of the world?

There are many answers to these questions, and within these answers are not only great challenges but also great opportunities, benefits, and gifts for all.

Einstein was at his usual level of brilliance when he said:

> **Significant problems cannot be solved**
> **on the same level of thinking**
> **that created the problems.**

This is a tremendous insight, one that affects every relationship we have. Nationally and internationally, we have become polarized; there are good guys and bad guys, liberals and conservatives, Christians and Muslims, friends and enemies. This divisiveness has led to demonizing other people, and has created a vast number of problems, resulting in endless struggle.

Einstein had it right: We cannot resolve our problems on the same divisive level they were created; we have to move to a higher perspective, one that allows us to talk to each other with respect. On this higher level of thought, we realize we all want the same things, ultimately: We all want peace, prosperity, and freedom to be ourselves. We all want respect. We all want our human rights honored and protected. Isn't that what you want? Isn't that what you want for your children?

The only way to solve our national and international problems is to work in partnership with *everyone*. To do this, we need to see one another as we really are: members of the same human family. We are all brothers and sisters, genetically and spiritually. Christ tells us exactly how to achieve this higher level of consciousness, in no uncertain terms:

Love your enemies.

I saw a great bumper sticker once that read, *Love your enemies. It'll drive them crazy.*

Let's at least try it and see what happens. A great many people are already working in partnership with all of humanity — and when we do we see wonderful — even magical — results.

We're beginning to see that it is possible, within our lifetimes, to create a world that works for all. Here's one way to express the key:

> Your focus creates your reality.
> You have the power to make this world
> a better place for all.

Affirm and repeat something like this (find appropriate words):

> I live in a world of peace and plenty,
> with abundance shared by all.
> I help make this world a world that works for all,
> where everyone on this sacred earth
> is housed, fed, healed, and educated
> so they can reach their greatest dreams.

So be it. So it is.

Our Relationship with Nature

We have a partnership with our Mother Earth that cannot be ignored; we have to treat her with love and respect. Are we consuming too many resources? Or even the right resources? Are we living in a sustainable way, within the means of the ecosystem?

What kind of world do we want to leave to our children, and their children, and all the generations to follow?

We already have, and have always had, a wonderful partnership with nature. She has given us so much, including life itself, and she has so much more to give us, including endless abundance and, far more importantly, the secrets of a life well lived.

Here's a key:

> **Your focus creates your reality.**
> **Focus on living in perfect harmony**
> **with all of sacred nature.**

Affirm and repeat something like this (find appropriate words for you):

> **Nature teaches me and guides me**
> **and shows me how to live,**
> **and how to fully realize what I am,**
> **as powerful as a mountain,**
> **as life giving as the sun.**

Our Relationship with Spirit

Are we in partnership with our spirit? Are we fully aware that we have a spiritual nature as well as a physical, emotional, and mental nature? Do we acknowledge and respect our spiritual side? Do we let it guide our lives? Do we respect the spiritual choices others have made?

These are the words I use at the beginning of my list of goals as affirmations — try repeating something like this, and see what happens:

> **Spirit flows through me every moment**
> **with its healing energy.**
> **I am guided by spirit, doing God's will.**
> **I offer no resistance to life,**

> I am at peace with what is,
> filled with grace, ease, and lightness.
> Every moment, I feel my Being.
> This is enlightenment.

So be it. So it is.

Here's one way to express this key to a fulfilling life:

> Your focus creates your reality.
> Realize who you are, in reality:
> You are a spiritual being
> having a physical experience.

Affirm something like this (find appropriate words for you):

> I am guided by spirit, every moment.
> I am a being of spirit, love, and light,
> now and forever.

So be it. So it is.

A Simple Key to Fulfilling Relationships

Let's review and sum up this whole chapter: To fully realize the life of our dreams, we have to apply the partnership model in every relationship we have. There is a simple key that can guide us, every day in every way:

Love and serve yourself and others
every day in every way.

Repeat that a few thousand times over the next few months, and see what happens. Miracles will follow miracles.

9

You Are the Tree of Life

The end of all wisdom
is love, love, love!

— Ramana Maharshi

Be not impatient in delay,
But wait as one who understands;
When spirit rises and commands,
The gods are ready to obey.

— Ella Wheeler Wilcox
(quoted by James Allen in *As You Think*)

The world itself and everything on it are magical creations. You can say that it's a miracle that it all exists. This isn't some religion you have to believe in or a philosophy that has no relevance in your daily life; this is simply what is. Our greatest scientists have come to the same conclusions as our mystics. Let's take another look at this brilliant insight of Einstein's that we saw earlier:

There are only two ways to live your life.
One is as though nothing is a miracle.
The other is as though everything is a miracle.
I choose the latter.

We choose how we view the world and ourselves. Our choice is usually an unconscious one, but we can choose to make our choices consciously. We can choose to see our world as a place composed of an endless series of miracles. We can choose to see ourselves as capable, creative individuals — capable, in fact, of creating miracles. The choice is up to us.

Take an honest look at yourself: Are you a hapless victim, at the mercy of forces beyond your control? Or are you a creator, able to shape your world by the power of your understanding and will?

The choice is yours to make — and the second choice is far closer to the truth of who you really are than the first one is. To paraphrase Hamlet: *There is far more in heaven and earth than any of us can dream of in our philosophies.* And we are far greater than any of us can fully understand. We are one with the whole of the endlessly creative cosmos, able to summon great forces into motion.

We have already discovered many ways to set those forces in motion. Reflecting on the Kabbalah is yet another way.

Reflections on the Kabbalah

Like many Western magical traditions, the Kabbalah seems at first to be endlessly long and complicated. A great many people have spent lifetimes studying it, and have gone into far greater depth than I have. But I'm not looking for erudite knowledge. I'm looking for simple, effective tools, for knowledge and practices that will change my life and my world in a short time. I'm looking for the short path, and I've found it in many places, including the Kabbalah.

The Kabbalah contains great truths about the force and course of magical creation. Some of the following comes from *The Tree of Life* by Israel Regardie — warm thanks to him for his work!

The Kabbalah studies the Tree of Life, with its ten stages, or *Sephiroth*. The Tree of Life is a map of creation — the creation of the cosmos, of our physical bodies, of anything we desire. We begin by reflecting on the roots of the tree — and in one sense the tree is inverted, upside down, because the roots of the Tree of Life are in heaven. The source of creation is in the highest realms of the spirit.

Here's an essential teaching of the Kabbalah:

> **All creation starts with a spiritual impulse,**
> **then becomes a thought, then an emotion.**
> **When thought and emotion are focused,**
> **physical creation is the result.**

The Kabbalah begins with the story of creation:

In the beginning is the endless void, shining pure infinity, symbolized by the number 0 — zero. Then the first miracle occurs: the One appears — a point of focus within this endless space.

This is the first Sephiroth, the Crown — the One, the infinite, the highest level of consciousness.

O

Then another wonderful miracle of creation occurs: the One becomes the Two. The second and third Sephiroth, the Father and the Mother, appear.

O

O   O

All of this takes place on the highest spiritual levels, in pure spirit, in very subtle forms, beyond description, in heaven, where the Tree of Life has its roots, its endless source.

The creative urge is now reflected to a denser level, a level we can describe and experience, for it is the level of thought, the mental realms. It reflects both the highest spiritual level of the One, and also the division of the One into the Two, the male and female. And now there are six Sephiroth....

O

SPIRITUAL REALMS

O   O

———————

O   O

MENTAL REALMS

O

Once creation is a thought, it has an energy that is powerful enough to become an emotion, and it is reflected to a still denser level. Creation has become a feeling, a desire. Again, the reflection contains both the focused One in the center, and its division into the Two, on the left and right....

                              O

SPIRITUAL REALMS
                        O   O

      _____

                        O   O

MENTAL REALMS
                              O

      _____

                        O   O

EMOTIONAL REALMS
                              O

And there are nine Sephiroth. Then, when spirit has become focused thought, and thought has become focused emotion, the energy of creation can move down the center of the Middle Pillar, without being pulled off course by moving to the left- or right-hand sides. When this happens, when focused thoughts are supported by unwavering positive feelings, the material plane becomes manifest — the physical plane we can see, touch, and feel — symbolized by the tenth Sephiroth:

```
                              O

      SPIRIT
                         O              O
     _____

                         O              O
      THOUGHT
                              O
     _____

                         O              O
      EMOTION
                              O
     _____


   PHYSICAL CREATION
                              O
```

The tenth Sephiroth is the realm of physical creation. It all begins with spirit, then becomes a focused thought, then a feeling, a desire, and finally it appears in physical reality.

The Tree of Life is composed of three powerful pillars. On the left is the feminine pillar, the divine female presence throughout the whole of creation. On the right is the male pillar, the divine male presence throughout the whole of creation. And through the center is the Middle Pillar, where the powers of the female and male are combined in perfect harmony, resulting in physical creation.

There is one great symbol — a symbol for both a planet and a gender — that connects and unifies the whole Tree of Life, one symbol that goes beyond all, one power, one energy that contains the whole of the force of creation and is the key to the mystery of life. Can you see it?

Look at the ten Sephiroth. Do you see that the top six form a circle? Make a circle that connects the top six. Then, from the sixth Sephiroth, make a straight line down thru the ninth and tenth. Then draw a horizontal line from the seventh to the eighth Sephiroth.

You have drawn the symbol for Venus, the symbol of woman, the symbol of the power of creation, the symbol of the power of love. *The end of all wisdom is love.*

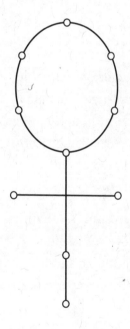

A new law I give to you:
Love one another, as I have loved you.

— JESUS

Lessons from the Kabbalah

What does it all mean? Is there really magical power in the study of this series of ten stages symbolizing various things? What can we learn from this in a way that affects our lives and our world?

The Kabbalah gives us a map of the process of creation, in the form of a simple diagram. All creation has a spiritual source; everything begins with a spiritual impulse. The one, single spiritual source of all of creation divides into two, the left and right, the male and female. Those two then become denser, and become thought, then become even denser and become emotion.

Both thought and emotion start with the stage of duality, where there is left and right, female and male. Then, if creation is to happen, both thought and emotion become single and focused. Then energy runs clearly down the center, the Middle Pillar of the Tree of Life, from spirit to thought to emotion to physical form.

This is a key to the creation of anything: Our thoughts need to be focused, and not wandering into left and right, whether into the dark areas of doubts and fears or into lighter, brighter areas where we consider other alternatives, or get distracted in other ways.

It's natural for us to first wander around and explore different ideas, different possible avenues available to us, but in order to create something, our thought has to become focused on a single, powerful idea.

Keep coming back to your focused thought.
Your focus creates your reality.

It's the same on the emotional level as well. As soon as we decide to create something, a great many feelings arise, good and bad. It's natural for anxieties to arise. The greater our dreams, the more doubts and fears arise. In order to create something, our emotions have to become focused as well as our thought.

And the greatest emotion — the emotion that is the most powerful in its ability to focus our thoughts and dreams — is the emotion of love.

Focus on your dreams with love,
and your dreams will soon become manifest.

Before long, you will be living in a world
that was only an insubstantial dream
a few years before.

Take a look at the drawing of the Tree of Life again, and look at it as a map of possible paths energy takes. Right down the center is the Middle Pillar. We've already been given this great key to magical creation: When your spiritual impulse becomes a focused thought, and is not distracted left or right, and when that focused thought becomes a focused feeling and, again, is not distracted left or right, the energy flows easily and effortlessly from spirit to thought to feeling to physical manifestation.

Keep focused on your dream. Don't let your thoughts wander for too long into doubt or hesitation; don't let your feelings wander for too long into fears, anxieties. Keep focused on the thought of your dream, your goal, your desire, whatever it is you want to create in your life. Keep filling those thoughts with love — as much love as you are capable of in the moment.

Remember who you really are — remember to feel your Presence, your Being. You are suspended in a vibrant field of light. You are that light. The light is life. The light is love.

> Take a deep breath, and let all thought go....
> Take another deep breath, and feel the light of your Presence....
> Feel the ocean of your Being....
>
> You are suspended in a vibrant field of light....
> You are that light....
> That light is life....
> That light is love.
>
> Dare to dream of what you want to create with love.

So be it. So it is!

10

Omnipotence and Eternity (and Other Great Things)

I have omnipotence at my command
and eternity at my disposal.

— Eliphas Lévi

Eliphas Lévi was a writer and magician in France in the 1800s. (Full disclosure: I haven't read a word of Lévi, other than the phrase that opens this chapter, which was quoted in *Moonchild*, a novel by Aleister Crowley that I really enjoyed, a magical battle between the forces of light and darkness.) His words touch on and contain the essence of magic. Let's read them again slowly, and ponder them a bit:

> I have omnipotence at my command
> and eternity at my disposal.

The phrase in itself is a powerful tool in a magician's mind. It is an affirmation, a declaration, and a summoning. The words have the power to summon the great forces they bring into focus: omnipotence and eternity.

Omnipotence

Omnipotence — all power. The power of all creation. It is at our command. As Ella Wheeler Wilcox put it:

> When spirit rises and commands,
> The gods are ready to obey.

What is the source of our omnipotence? Those of us who were raised as Christians were given a simple way to understand it when we were children: God, we were taught, is *omnipotent, omniscient, and omnipresent* — all-powerful, all-knowing, and present everywhere. Since God is everywhere, God is obviously in every atom of every cell of our bodies. We are part of God.

The power of God infuses every cell of our bodies as well as every atom of the universe. We are a microcosm reflecting the whole macrocosm; we are an essential part of creation, eternally connected to the source of creation and the whole of creation.

We have omnipotence at our command; we only need to summon it, and we become aware that we are filled, every moment, with the endless creative energy of the universe.

An ancient teaching from India puts it even more simply:

Thou art That.

You are That — all that is. The microcosm and the macrocosm are one. You are one with the whole universe, filled with the creative energy of the universe. It is at your disposal, at your command, because it is you, you are it.

Eternity

We have a physical body and a spiritual body. The physical body dies, but in our spiritual bodies, we live forever. We have eternity at our disposal. The Bhagavad Gita put it very clearly, five thousand years ago:

**There never was a time when you didn't exist;
there will never be a time when you don't exist.**

The Magician in the Tarot deck has the symbol of eternity over his head. That picture of the Magician is a picture of us. We raise our right hand and summon the creative forces of the universe; we point to the earth with our left hand and command the creation of our dreams.

THE MAGICIAN.

We have the symbol of eternity above us: We live and grow eternally, becoming ever more awakened, more powerful, and more peaceful.

> We are endlessly evolving,
> and we can consciously speed up the process,
> becoming ever more awakened,
> more powerful, and more peaceful.

The Power of an Altar

People have known about the power of altars as long as there have been people on earth. Place any image or images on your altar that you wish — things you find beautiful and inspiring. Find an image or images that remind you of what you know:

You are a powerful, creative force of nature, first imagining and then actually creating the life of your dreams.

Your altar can be large or small. It can have one image or dozens of statues, pictures, mandalas, candles, incense, trinkets, mementos. It can be as simple or as elaborate as you want to make it.

Give your altar some attention in some way on a regular (or, if you're like me, highly sporadic) basis. Develop your own way to relate to it. Pray to the images on it, or meditate with them.

When you relax, when you meditate, one option you have is to visualize or imagine your inner altar — the altar you create in your mind. My inner altar is vast, with many, many images from many traditions. (I'm into spiritual soup, as you may have noticed.) I scan over my altar and pick the image I want to remember, focus on, pray to, or summon in the moment.

INNER ALTAR MEDITATION

Find a place where you can be quiet and alone. Sit or lie comfortably. Loosen your belt; turn off your cell phone.

Take a deep breath, and as you slowly exhale, relax your body, from head to toe....
Take another deep breath, and as you slowly exhale, relax your mind, and let all thought go....
Take another deep breath, and let it all go....
It feels so good to deeply relax....
Feel your presence within:
Feel yourself suspended in a vibrant field of light....

Relax, and let yourself float in an ocean of light, life, and love....

Imagine that there is a beautiful altar in front of you.... Perhaps it just has one image on it, or a few things in a pleasing arrangement, or perhaps it's a long altar, extending off to the left and the right, filled with many different statues and images....

Scan through the various images on your altar, and pick one to focus on. Bring that image to mind, as clearly as possible....
Feel the energy that radiates from that image....
Feel the wordless connection you have....

You are summoning the power and the grace of the image you have chosen....
Let its power and grace fill your being....
Let the words of a prayer come to mind....

What you do next is up to you. You can engage in a dialogue with the image you have summoned. You can ask questions, and listen for answers. Or you can have a quiet, wordless communion with that image....

You have omnipotence at your command. You are capable of bringing the energy of the divine, the ultimate creative forces of the universe, into your sphere of awareness....

Now focus clearly on what you want to create in your life. Ask for it. Pray for it....
Feel the power of the image in front of you....
Let its power and support fill every cell of your body....

Affirm your dreams are coming into being,
in an easy and relaxed manner,
a healthy and positive way,
in its own perfect time,
for the highest good of all.

This, or something better, is now manifesting, for the highest good of all....

So be it. So it is.

The Power of Amulets and Printed Prayers

Wearing an amulet and surrounding yourself with printed prayers are also powerful magical tools that have been used for thousands of years throughout the world. Like all the other tools, they help us remember; they help us imprint our prayers, desires, and dreams into our subconscious mind. Then the real magic begins.

Many cultures make and wear amulets; some are very simple, some more elaborate. Some students of Tibetan Buddhism are given an amulet to wear that contains a single sheet of paper, folded many times: a print of a mandala, with Buddha at the center, surrounded by prayers. The piece of paper is perhaps ten inches square, and is folded and put into a sewn silk container about three inches square. It has a simple string necklace, worn over the center of the chest.

Wearing the amulet is a constant reminder that you have the mind and nature of Buddha — vast, all-encompassing, eternally light. It is a reminder that you are an enlightened being, a reminder of the nature of your mind.

Tibetans certainly understand the power of the printed word. They surround themselves with prayer flags and *thankas* — paintings of mandalas — and large and small prayer wheels. At the Nyingma Tibetan Center in Berkeley, we printed thousands and thousands of prayers on long rolls of paper four or five feet wide. In the basement were several large pipes, maybe four inches in diameter, and we wrapped each one with layer after layer of prayers (working many hours at it, always at night) so the paper formed a cylinder at least two feet thick. The cylinders were motorized to spin at high velocity, twenty-four hours a day, sending millions and millions of prayers into the quantum field every day.

Many times the entire sheet of prayers is just covered with a single, great prayer:

Om Mani Padme Hum!

Om is the single sound of the universe, the sound that unites you with the quantum field. *Mani* is the jewel of bliss that resides in our minds. *Padme* is the lotus of consciousness, rising from the mud to blossom in the sun. *Hum* is the syllable that makes it all happen — and we realize the jewel of bliss in the lotus of our consciousness.

Another simple practice is to write your own prayer repeatedly on a sheet of paper and post it on your wall, or carry it around with you.

For years, I've had this page on my office wall:

I achieve my dreams,
in an easy and relaxed manner,
a healthy and positive way,
in its own perfect time,
for the highest good of all.

This, or something better,
is now manifesting,
in totally satisfying
and harmonious ways,
for the highest good of all.

So be it. So it is!

I achieve my dreams,
in an easy and relaxed manner,
a healthy and positive way,
in its own perfect time,
for the highest good of all,
I pray.

This, or something better,
is now manifesting,
in totally satisfying
and harmonious ways,
for the highest good of all.

So be it. So it is!

I achieve my goals,
in an easy and relaxed manner,
a healthy and positive way,
in its own perfect time,
for the highest good of all.

This, or something better,
is now manifesting,
in totally satisfying
and harmonious ways,
for the highest good of all.

So be it. So it is!

I am living the life of my dreams,
in an easy and relaxed manner,
a healthy and positive way,
in its own perfect time,
for the highest good of all,
I pray.

This, or something better,
is now manifesting,
in totally satisfying
and harmonious ways,
for the highest good of all.

So be it. So it is!

Find the ways that work for you to keep your dreams in mind. You have an endless number of alternatives.

Making a Love Charm

A great many traditions have love charms, and I include this only because I made and used a simple charm years ago that definitely had a positive effect on several people, including me.

I wandered through the "stacks" — the archives — of an old library one time at the University of Minnesota and found two remarkable books about the Gypsy culture — the Romany — in Europe in the early 1900s. One of the books had story after story about Gypsy healers. Using herbs, prayers, and charms, they often cured diseases and ailments that medical doctors had failed to cure. One of the stories was about a boy who had been blind from birth, and was told his blindness was permanent — and an old Gypsy woman cured him by washing out his eyes and repeatedly applying a poultice filled with herbs. His full sight was restored.

Gypsies, Wiccans — those who have practiced wicca, or witchcraft, in some form — and indigenous people all over the world have powerful healing traditions using herbs and other natural ingredients. Personally, I trust herbal healing far more than chemical medicine. The few times I've found it necessary to get some medical attention, I've gone to a Chinese doctor who uses herbs and acupuncture — proven medicinal practices over five thousand years old.

Herbs are tried and true, with little or no negative side effects. Prescription drugs are the developments of a relatively new technology, and I avoid them completely. But I digress — and I am not offering medical advice of any kind. I do want to suggest, though, that you are your own best healer. Trust your body's natural healing processes: The human species has been evolving for several million years, and our bodies' healing systems are powerful, especially when we relax and remove as much stress as possible, and let our healing systems do their phenomenal job.

The other old book I found in the stacks of the library in Minnesota had several Gypsy charms written out, transcribed from their language, the Romany or Rom language — a sister language to Sanskrit and Latin. One was a love charm.

I was young and single at the time, so I wrote a copy of it and folded it up. At first, I just carried it around with me. Later on, I put it in a little pouch made from a wide piece of ribbon that had been doubled over and sewn up. I added a dab of rosemary oil to the paper, and put a few sprigs of rosemary into it as well. (Rosemary, it is said in some traditions, has the power to attract lovers.) My love life definitely became more energized when I carried that amulet around!

I met a woman named Ginger, a single mother who was fascinated with the story behind the love charm: If you go to a willow tree at midnight on New Year's Eve and shake the tree as you repeat the chant — shaking it hard enough so that some leaves fall (this must assume you're in a climate warm enough that willow trees still have leaves in winter) — then a white dog will bark, and your true love will come to you. Before next New Year's Eve will fall, you'll be wedded and bedded and all.

Ginger learned the words, and went at midnight on the next New Year's Eve and shook a willow tree and repeated the chant. She shook vigorously until some leaves fell, and then stopped. She waited awhile; nothing happened.

A few weeks later, she had a picnic lunch with her daughter right near the willow tree, and she noticed a white dog barking, over and over. Then a tall, dark, good-looking man came sauntering up to her and said, "Ginger?" He turned out to be an old friend from high school she hadn't seen in years. And before the next New Year's Eve, they were wedded and bedded and all.

Here are the words — they have music in them when they're chanted. I set them to music, and added some English words — a loose interpretation of the original ancient words of the Rom.

A LOVE CHARM

Per de, per de prajtina
Varakaj heen has kamov
Baso paro dzui u klo
Perano dzal may dzigo

New Year's Eve, a willow tree
Where will my true lover be?
Shake the tree, shake the tree
When will my love come to me?

Many earths on earth there be,
Who I love my own shall be
Grow, grow, willow tree
No sorrow unto thee!
No sorrow unto me!

Scattered leaves around I see
Who I love my own shall be
Ah, the white dog barks at last
And my love comes running fast

Thank you, Lord, for now I hold
My lover with your charms of old
Before next New Year's Eve will fall
I'll be wedded and bedded and all.

Per de, per de prajtina
Varakaj heen has kamov
Baso paro dzui u klo
Perano dzal may dzigo

The Power of a Star

The five-pointed star has been associated with various forms of magic for thousands of years. It represents the body of man and woman: the five points are the head, the outstretched arms, and the wide-set legs.

The star is a mandala, a representation of the entire universe as well. Each one of us is a star; each one of us reflects and represents the whole of the universe as well.

The six-pointed star, most often associated with Judaism, is a powerful magical symbol as well. It contains the whole of the Kabbalah, in a way, for it is composed of two great equilateral triangles: one with its base at the bottom, representing all of creation, and one with its base at the top, its energy radiating downward, representing the spirit and energy of the whole universe infusing the whole of creation with light and life, creating form out of emptiness.

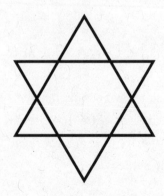

You can access the power of a star through meditation and visualization, and through drawing the star on paper as well.

STAR MEDITATION

Take a deep breath, close your eyes, and relax....
Take another deep breath, and let all thought go as you exhale....
Take another deep breath, and as you exhale, let everything go, so that you're floating in a sea of light, bathed in the light of a star....

Now imagine that you are a star....
Imagine that, in front of you, is a warm glowing field of light — a star!
Imagine that you are part of that light. Feel it penetrate and fill every cell of your body....
Feel it — and know that is who and what you are. You are a star!

Imagine in your mind's eye a blazing star in front of you....
It has arms of radiant light coming out of it — five or six or any number of brilliant extensions of radiant light....
Let each of these parts of the star represent a part of your life....

At the top is your eternal connection with spirit. Immerse yourself in that light, and affirm something like:

> Spirit flows through me every moment
> with its healing energy.
> I am guided by spirit, every moment,
> doing God's will.
> I am at peace with what is,
> filled with grace, ease, and lightness.
> Every moment, I feel my being.
> This is enlightenment.

Feel the light from the top of the star — the light of God, grace, creation, whatever you want to call it — permeate every cell of your being....

At the other points of light radiating from your star, place your other dreams, hopes, and goals, and affirm each one into being....

Don't forget the part of the radiant star that is about family and friendships. Affirm something like:

> My marriage, family life, and friendships
> are filled with grace, ease, and lightness.
> So be it. So it is.

You might want to make a drawing of a star as well, and keep it in your Magician's Toolkit. At every point of the star, have your dreams, goals, prayers, affirmations. You are in a very powerful way bringing the creative power of the universe to your dreams and goals.

So be it. So it is.

One-Minute Yoga

Yoga means "union." It's similar to the English word *yoke* — through yoga we reunite with our spiritual nature. (The word *religion* is similar to *yoga*: The root is probably the Latin word *ligare*, which means to "bind" or "connect." Through religion we reconnect with the sacred.)

I'm extremely lazy, and my bouts of yoga are brief. One minute of yoga can still make a big difference in your day or night.

> Stand up, stretch your arms high, and then do a minute of yoga, like a Salute to the Sun, or any other physical movements that feel good in the moment.

If yoga stretches turn into just some form of plain old exercise movements, that's just fine.

Now, as one teacher in India put it,

> **Close your eyes
> and see God.**

Finally,

> **Open your eyes
> and see God
> everywhere.**
>
> **Omnipresent
> Omniscient
> Omnipotent**

> Present everywhere
> All knowing
> All powerful

The Days of the Week

There is a magic, a power, in the names we've given the days of the week. It's archetypal, in some deeply beautiful way. Don't let your rational thinking tell you it's just all arbitrary nonsense. The days of the week were named after the five planets known thousands of years ago, which were all named after gods and goddesses of Greece and Rome. It's part of the study of astrology, which some people enjoy (including me) and other people find to be nonsense (which is fine — a study of astrology is certainly not necessary). Johannes Kepler, a key figure in our scientific revolution, put it this way:

> **No one should hold it to be incredible that**
> **out of the astrologer's foolishness and blasphemies**
> **some useful and sacred knowledge may come.**

There is certainly some useful and sacred knowledge in the names of the days of the week. Each one represents a different sacred force, and reflecting on that force throughout the day can be useful, even powerful.

SUNDAY is of course named for the Sun. It is a perfect day for rejuvenation; relax, get outside if the weather is good. Have a day of rest during the week — even God needed a day of rest! It's a good day for family and friends; it's a day of sunny dispositions.

MONDAY is Moon Day. It's the worst day of the week, in my opinion, to start a workweek. The Moon is associated with emotions, and Monday is often emotional, a great day for reflection, quiet. It can be a day of intuitive breakthroughs and discovery. Try to work as little as possible. Get in a hot tub or take a hot bath in the evening. Look at the moon for a while. It might have some messages for you.

TUESDAY is Mars's Day. It's interesting that in English, some of the days are named after Norse or Germanic gods and goddesses. Tuesday is named for the Germanic god Tiu. Latin languages use the Roman names; in French, Tuesday is *mardi* (*martes* in Spanish, *martedì* in Italian) — Mars Day. Now this is a good day to start a workweek! You have the power and energy of Mars behind you. It's great for action in the world, and launching creative ideas — just avoid some people's tendencies to get into conflicts when there's too much Mars energy, too much testosterone.

Too much testosterone — an excess of Mars energy — may be the single greatest cause of most of the world's major problems. Natural male aggression has to be balanced with some softer energies, like compassion and love. When Mars energy and Venus energy work together, magical creation happens.

WEDNESDAY is Mercury Day — or *mercredi* in French — named for the Germanic god Odin (or Wotan). It's a great day for communication, mental work, taking care of business, writing, visiting, meetings.

THURSDAY is Thor's Day — or *jeudi* in French: Jupiter Day. An expansive day, a day of growth, creativity, positive encounters. A good day for meetings. (I always try to schedule my meetings on Thursday; Wednesday is my second choice. And never on Monday!) People are often in a good mood on Thursdays.

FRIDAY — or *vendredi* in French — is Venus Day. The English word is named after Frigga, a Germanic goddess roughly equivalent to Venus. Celebrate the feminine, the compassion and vision of womankind. Go to someplace beautiful. No wonder Friday night is date night! Love relationships can bloom. It's also great for creative expression and settling difficulties. It's a day of love.

> The day will come when,
> after harnessing space,
> the winds, the tides, and gravitation,
> we shall harness for God the energies of love.
> And, on that day, for the second time in the
> history of the world,
> we shall have discovered fire.
>
> — TEILHARD DE CHARDIN

SATURDAY is Saturn's Day (we're back to the Roman gods). As Jupiter is associated with expansion, Saturn is associated with contraction. A good day to complete things, take care of details. Saturn is also ruler of Capricorn, the sign associated with accomplishment and mastery: This is a good day to remember to focus on your dreams, and take another step toward becoming a master of your life.

The Months of the Year

Throughout the week, we have the rhythm of the days; throughout the year, we have the rhythm of the months. Each has an ancient astrological name and sign, and there is a deep meaning in each one.

On a very practical level, an awareness of the different months of the year and the different signs they represent is an awareness of the seasons: the expansiveness of spring and summer; the contraction of fall and winter. And each month through the year has its own rhythm, alternating between active, male, yang energy and quieter, more reflective, female, yin energy.

JANUARY begins with the celebration of the New Year, and is a time for new plans, new beginnings. It is the month of Capricorn, which rules the midheaven — the tenth house in astrology, directly over our heads, the zenith, the highest position of the sun. It is the sign of the master. Hone your mastery: This can be a month of preparation and growth that leads to effortless accomplishment. Capricorn is ruled by Saturn, who represents the wisdom that grows with age.

This growth can't be forced, however. We are in the middle of winter, a season of stillness and rest. It is a time to do the planning, the inner work, that will come to fruition later in the year.

FEBRUARY is the depth of winter, yet for most of the month the sun is in the sign of Aquarius, the water bearer, the visionary and futurist. It can be a month of new ideas, surprises, and light amidst the darkness of winter. It's a great month to expand your plans and dreams — are you dreaming big enough?

MARCH is the end of winter, the month of Pisces. This is a good time not to force things, or plan on great results; this is a good time to go within, relax, and reflect, for the month is the deep, mysterious transfiguration from winter to spring. Pisces is the last sign, the culmination of the entire cycle of the year. It is the sign of ultimate understanding. It is the sign of the mystic, a time for stillness and silence, a time to discover the deepest inner wonder of it all.

Don't try to do too much outer activity this month. Read and reflect. (Highly recommended for this month: Eckhart Tolle's *Stillness Speaks*.)

APRIL — finally, spring bursts forth, with its rush of high, creative energy. This is the real New Year, because life bursts forth once again in all its glory. It's the month of Aries — a great time to launch new projects, try new ideas, get out in the world, take risks, and let your spirit soar. There is a great energy this month: Aries is ruled by Mars. Dare to dream — and go for it!

MAY is the month of Taurus, the bull. Let things slow down a bit, find a deeper, slower rhythm, a time for grounding, growing roots, connecting with the powerful sustaining energies of the Earth. This is a month to lay the groundwork to realize your vision. There is a great beauty in this month: Taurus is ruled by Venus.

JUNE is the month of Gemini, another high-energy month like April. Ruled by Mercury, it's great for communication, writing, expressing your vision, doing your work in the world. A good month to sharpen and skillfully use the power of your mind. A good month to get out in the world and make things happen.

JULY is the wonderful height of summer, the month of the sign of Cancer (or, as I prefer to call it, the Moonchild). It's ruled by the Moon, and people's energy often settles down again, after the excitement of the month of Gemini. July is a great time to be home, grounded, growing. A time to turn inward for your answers, and reflect on the baseline happiness that is within you, beyond your thoughts and feelings. A time to celebrate and appreciate your home and family and the fullness of life.

AUGUST is the month of Leo, ruled by the Sun. The intense Sun brings people out into the light, and it is a great time to share, travel, relate, perform. Put on a show! Realize your dream. You are a star — so let your light shine.

SEPTEMBER — summer withdraws, fall is upon us. The month of Virgo is ruled by Mercury, and is a wonderful time to get your house in order, and your business and creative life as well, a time to organize, and — most of all — to love and serve yourself and others, and remember who you really are and what you're here to do.

OCTOBER is the beautiful month of Libra, ruled by Venus. Fall bursts forth in all its many colors; this is a time of inspiration, of connecting with others, of being bountiful and beautiful, creating beauty and harmony around you.

NOVEMBER is the month of Scorpio. Winter is upon us, often quite suddenly. It is darker much earlier in the day. Scorpio has the stinging power of the scorpion in its unevolved state, the healing energy of the snake winding up the spine (symbolized by the caduceus, the staff carried by Mercury) in its evolving state, and the vision of the eagle in its evolved state. When you meditate in this month, you can easily sense the healing energy that moves up and down your spine, and you can discover within your third eye the vision of an eagle.

Scorpio has the twin power of Mars — strength and fire — connected with Pluto, the ultimate, the beyond. This is a month of great depth, a time to meditate and reflect, but (like the month of Pisces) not a time to attempt to accomplish a great deal, at least in the outer world. Relax, rejuvenate, go within.

DECEMBER is the month of Sagittarius, ruled by Jupiter, expansive, jovial. There's a strong, boisterous, outgoing energy this month, beginning with Thanksgiving in late November and building to the winter solstice celebrated in so many ways by so many traditions, including, of course, Christmas and Hanukkah. Celebrate abundance all month — from Thanksgiving on. Another year has ended, and we all have so much to be grateful for.

Celebrate what is. Reflect on Eckhart Tolle's words:

> **Gratitude for the present moment**
> **and the fullness of life now**
> **is true prosperity.**

So be it. So it is!

A Brief Summary

We have omnipotence at our command and eternity at our disposal. We are endlessly evolving, and we can consciously speed up the process by remembering, over and over, by any means necessary, to reconnect with our spirit, with the source of all our power, the source of all creation.

11

The Mystical and Spiritual Side of Success

We will never understand the forces of creation.
But we can set them in motion —
and then sit back in wonder
at the mystery and majesty of it all.

The magical, the mystical, the spiritual — all are interlinked. Magical practice connects with spiritual power; the results can be startling, and can happen quickly — that's why it's called a short path. The process is a mystical one that we can never fully understand. It will always remain a mystery.

Eckhart Tolle said scientists will be studying the human body a thousand years from now and will still be asking new questions and uncovering new mysteries. It is certainly true of the process of creation as well: We will never understand it fully. But we can understand it enough to set it in motion — it just takes a moment — and then we sit back in wonder at the mystery and beauty of it all.

I've written and talked many times before on the many different spiritual paths to success.* Is there really, truly a short path we can take? Let's reflect on something for a while and see where it leads us. Let's look at a way of seeing the world that is both simple to understand and profound in its implications.

Outer, Inner, and Secret Forms of Existence

This is something I learned from a Tibetan teacher many years ago: Everything has outer, inner, and secret levels of being or forms of existence; each one is different, and an awareness of each brings us great understanding and wisdom — and, yes, even *enlightenment*.

Take the chair you might be sitting in at the moment as an example: In its outer form, it's simply a chair, made of wood (or whatever). It's solid, covered with paint or colored cloth, and built in a way that supports you as you sit in it.

What is its inner form? If it's made of wood, it has a great many wooden fibers within, seemingly solid. When you go

---

* The spiritual path to success is the subject of the eleventh chapter of *Visionary Business* and the eleventh chapter of *The Millionaire Course*; it's also the title of the eleventh session in the *Success with Ease* audio series, and is available as a separate audio download (*The Spiritual Path to Success*) as well.

more deeply into its inner form, however, you find it is composed of billions of cells, which are composed of trillions of molecules, bound together — working in a great, miraculous partnership — to create the outer form of the chair. Going even deeper, to the atomic level, you find it's mostly empty space, filled with whirling energy and mysterious information.

What is its secret level of being? It can be expressed in many different ways. Here's one way to put it: That chair is a microcosm reflecting the macrocosm of the entire universe. The creation of that chair involves the same forces as the creation of the whole universe. The chair is a mandala: a picture, a chart of the whole process and result of creation.

It shows us something Buddhists have been chanting for about 2,500 years:

**Form is emptiness;
emptiness is form.**

It shows us that the emptiness and form of the chair are completely connected with everything else in the universe. We are all one.

Let's look at our bodies as another example: In their outer form, our bodies have a solid, physical presence in the world. They have a specific color and shape that we can easily see (unless we're blind). They are capable of a wide range of motion and movement. They can do and build all kinds of things. They can be bent, broken, smashed, and mutilated. They will eventually wear out and die and decompose. (This reminds me of a joke: *What has Beethoven been doing for the past two hundred years? Decomposing.*)

What is their inner form, however? A complex system of organs and other systems all doing their necessary work to keep the body running smoothly. And when we go more deeply into the body's inner form, we find it's composed of roughly a trillion cells, working together in amazing complexity and harmony. These cells are composed of trillions of molecules, composed of atoms. Going even deeper, we find it's empty space, filled with energy and information and mystery.

What is the secret level of being of our bodies? It could be expressed this way: Your body is a microcosm reflecting the macrocosm of the whole universe. The creation of your body involves the same forces as the creation of the universe. Your body is a mandala: a picture, a chart of the whole process of creation.

As above, so below.

Your outer and inner forms are temporary, and will soon pass away, but at its core, in its essence, your body consists of the energy of life, and is one with all that is. It is an energy that will not fade, for it cannot be created or destroyed. It simply is. And it always will be.

Repeat this mantra — these words of power — again: *Form is emptiness; emptiness is form.* The emptiness and form of our bodies are completely connected with everything else in the universe. We are all one, now and forever.

When we reflect on this secret level of being, we realize the miracle and magic of our bodies, and of our existence. Once we truly understand this, we realize who we are — and we are enlightened. We are self-realized. We are in awe of the wonder of *what is.*

> **Underneath the level of physical appearances**
> **and separate forms,**
> **you are one with all that is.**
>
> — ECKHART TOLLE, *The Power of Now*

Success, Abundance, Fulfillment

Now let's turn our attention to success, abundance, and fulfillment. One of the simplest and yet most powerful ways to achieve all of these is to reflect on what those words mean for us, and clearly imagine and state what they mean for us in their outer, inner, and secret forms.

Once we can imagine something clearly, the steps to take to create it become obvious. Start with defining — imagining — what outer success means for you, then inner success. On a secret level, of course, you are absolutely perfect right now in this moment; you're one with all that is. There is nothing you have to do. You are complete.

> **You are an eternal part of an eternal creation,**
> **a quintessential piece of divine revelation.**

Outer Success

Outer success — what does that mean for you? You are a unique, creative person, and your definition of your success is probably not what your parents wanted for themselves or what they want for you. It's not what anyone else thinks it should be. You, and you alone, can define what success means for you.

Perhaps you already know exactly what you want in life. If you don't, it's something to pray for, something to ask for guidance about. If you don't have a clear, concrete picture of what you want in life, do the Ideal Scene Meditation in chapter 1, or do a shorter version like this:

Sit comfortably and relax....
Close your eyes, and become aware of your breathing. Let your breaths become longer and deeper as you relax more deeply....
Relax your body, from head to toe....
Relax your mind, let all thought go....
Let everything go....
Relax into the vibrant field of light within....

Now picture your dream life, two or three or five years in the future. What are you doing on most of your days? What does your environment look like? What have you attained?

Ask to be guided by spirit, every moment of every day; ask to be led to first picture — imagine — the perfect life for you, the highest dream you can imagine....

Now ask to see the next steps to take to create your perfect life of perfect fulfillment....

Be quiet, relax, and see what comes up for you....

Define your outer success as clearly and concretely as you can. Does it mean the freedom to travel or write or teach or create something? Does it mean a family? Does it mean a specific amount of money in the bank? Does it include real estate? How much leisure time do you have? Do you want a life that's easy, relaxed, healthy, positive? Define clearly what you want.

Then simply ask for it in your prayers. Or affirm repeatedly it is now coming into being, in an easy and relaxed manner, a healthy and positive way, in its own perfect time, for the highest good of all. That might be all you need to do on the magical path — the direct path to fulfillment.

Affirm something like this:

**I am guided by spirit
every moment.**

**I am guided by spirit
to find and fulfill
my calling, my vocation.**

**I am guided by spirit
to grow into my potential,
and realize the life of my dreams.
So be it. So it is!**

Or even something like this:

> I do wonderful work
> in a wonderful way
> with wonderful people
> for wonderful pay.

Keep asking for inner guidance, and then let plans emerge. Write them down. Have a concrete goal at the top of each one of your plans. Take the next obvious steps in front of you toward reaching those goals you have in writing. Take one small step at a time; the longest journey, climbing the highest mountain, consists of a series of small, doable steps.

Don't dream too small. You'll never regret going for your dreams!

> Make no little plans;
> they have no magic to stir your blood....
> Make big plans; aim high in hope and work.
>
> — DANIEL BURNHAM, architect and urban planner

Inner Success

Some of us get into conflicts within ourselves about achieving outer success because we know, in our hearts, that there are far more important things in life than our accomplishments in the world and the things we surround ourselves with. As long as we're in conflict about it, we can sabotage ourselves, in both outer and inner success.

Don't be afraid to go for outer success — it's not only for your highest good, after all, but for the highest good of all as well. Keep affirming it, and it is true:

> **This, or something better,**
> **is now manifesting,**
> **in totally satisfying and harmonious ways,**
> **for the highest good of all.**
>
> **So be it. So it is.**

If we keep affirming those words, the words have the power to overcome a lot of the fears that prevent us from being fulfilled, content with our lives, and reaching our greatest good in this big, wide, magical world we live in.

We know that true success in the outer world has to include the inner things we know are important, for they're essential to happiness and to a life well lived.

What does inner success mean to you? Most people want the same things here: happiness — as much as possible — inner peace, satisfaction, fulfillment, serenity. (There are exceptions — I just heard a woman from New York City say, "I'm not into yoga or health food or serenity." I'm certain, though, that she would like to be happy in life, satisfied, fulfilled in some way. Don't all of us want that?)

Spend some time reflecting on this. What internal state of body and mind do you want to achieve? And how can you achieve it?

Affirmations, mantras, magical formulas — call them what you will — are powerful in affecting our inner states of being. They are the magical tools we use on the short path to realization. Keep finding the right words to affirm, especially when there are challenges and difficulties. Find your own words; here are some suggestions:

I am enough, I am complete.
I have everything I need
to enjoy my here and now.

I am guided by spirit every moment,
doing what I love.

My marriage, family life, and career are filled with grace,
ease, and lightness.

Spirit flows through me every moment
with its healing energy.
I am guided by spirit, doing God's will.
I offer no resistance to life,
I am at peace with what is,
and I am filled with grace, ease, and lightness.
Every moment, I feel my Being.
This is enlightenment.

The Secret of Success

There is a great secret here that is no secret at all. People have been saying it for many thousands of years, but it makes no sense to most people, for it seems to completely contradict the obvious truths of their lives of struggle and hardship and unrealized hopes and dreams.

It can be expressed in many different ways, of course — and so, before I put it in my words, it might be good to ask yourself these questions and ponder the answers that come to mind:

What is truly important in life?
What is lasting and meaningful?
What is the secret of success, for me?

Here are the words that come to my mind, at this moment, when I ask those questions: What is truly important in life? Understanding *what is*. What is lasting and meaningful? Life, which is endless and eternal. Life, which is light and love.

What is the secret of success? You are already fully, wonderfully complete and successful as you are, just by being alive in this moment. Dream your dreams and go for them, but never forget that you are perfect as you are, and this moment is perfect as it is.

A Tibetan teacher named Long Chen Pa (also written as Longchenpa) wrote some words about a thousand years ago that have become famous around the world. He taught what he called *Dzogchen*, meaning "absolute perfection." (One reason I like him is that in the middle of his great teaching career — he had thousands of students — he took twelve years off and meditated in a cave.) He wrote a book — *The Natural Freedom of Mind* — and it has this passage:

Since everything is an illusion,
perfect in being what it is,
having nothing to do with good or bad,
or whether we accept it or reject it,
one may well burst out in laughter.

Everything is perfect in being what it is — that includes you and me and the whole universe. There is nothing we need to attain — we simply need to realize the wonder, the magic, the miracle of who and what we are. We are life itself!

The Spiritual Path of Prayer

I hope you have seen by now that prayer works. Prayer is a powerful form of magic; the short path is through prayer. You don't have to believe it — just try it, with an open heart and mind, and see what happens. Prayer works — unless we undo our prayers in our next series of thoughts.

Prayer, affirmations, declarations, mantras, chants, magical formulas, positive thinking, strategic planning: They all work. Negative thinking works just as well, unfortunately, so watch what you think!

Negative thinking is just as powerfully creative as positive thinking. That's been proven the world over. But it's also true that the right prayer, the right affirmation, the right positive thought, can overcome weeks, months, years — even decades — of negative thinking.

Let the past go. It's over and done with. All we have is this moment now. In this moment, pray for what you want.

**Dare to dream and affirm the highest,
most wonderful life you can imagine.**

> **Our thoughts and prayers of today
> determine our life in the future.**

So be it. So it is!

The Spiritual Path to Success

Through trial and error, I've come to see this: If you do understand that we all have a spiritual life, it can be the quickest, most direct route to success — whatever success means for you.

This entire book could be called *The Spiritual Path to Success*, because the spiritual path and the magical path are one. Guided by spirit, we first create something in our minds, and then it becomes manifest on the physical plane.

Our outer world is filled with great, solid structures that are the genius and fulfillment of humankind as well as the genius and fulfillment and intelligent design of a power far greater than humankind. Everything created was first an inner creation — an idea, a focused thought.

And the greatest of these creations originate in spirit. Spirit is the loving, compassionate source of all creation. And we have a direct link to it at every moment.

> **Ask and it will be given you.
> Seek and you will find.
> Knock, and it will be opened unto you,**

> For everyone who asks, receives,
> and those who seek, find,
> and to those who knock
> it will be opened.
>
> — MATTHEW 7:7–8

The answers are within the stillness and the quiet voice of your spirit. Go within. Just take one deep breath, and relax and close your eyes....

Go within.
Let all thought go....

Feel your Presence.
Feel the light within you.

This is the plane of magical creation.
This is the plane of spiritual revelation.

12

CREATING A WORLD THAT WORKS FOR ALL

It is the intention of this course
to assist in the growth of a peaceful army
of visionaries, artists, entrepreneurs, businesspeople,
teachers, writers, activists, and leaders
who are transforming not only their own lives
but the whole world as well,
creating a world that works for all,
in an easy and relaxed manner,
a healthy and positive way,
in its own perfect time,
for the highest good of all.

We have all the tools we need now. The process remains a mystery, but we know how to set it in motion. We've already seen remarkable changes in our lives; now it's time to create some remarkable changes in our world as well. The same magical tools that work to create the life of our dreams are the tools we can use to make the world a far better place when we leave it than when we arrived here.

The process to make major changes in the world is the same process we used to make major changes in our lives: First, we dare to dream of a world that works for all, then we imagine possibilities, and then we make plans and take the first small steps. We affirm the dream with the power of the spoken word, and we realize the dream with the power of the written word and committed action.

> **Never doubt that a small group**
> **of thoughtful, committed people**
> **can change the world.**
> **Indeed, it is the only thing that ever has.**
>
> — MARGARET MEAD

There is a rapid route — a direct path — to changing the world for the better. As more of us realize this, change can and will happen quickly.

The Dream

We have to start with a dream. Then we imagine how we can possibly achieve it. We brainstorm, make lists of *What Ifs*. We discuss different possibilities. Then we make clear goals and make plans to reach those goals. We take the first steps in front of us. And we change the world.

So few people dare to dream of a better world. And yet that's exactly what is needed on a global basis now: a large number of people (even though, as Margaret Mead reminds us, it can be a remarkably small percentage of the population) who have a vision of a world that works for all, and are doing something to realize that vision.

The most important thing to keep in mind, always, is the dream, the vision:

Keep the dream, the vision, in mind:
It is possible to create a world that works for all,
where all are fed, housed, and educated.
This is the Great Work ahead of us.

The great visionary and pioneer Buckminster Fuller realized this many decades ago. He said back in the 1960s that we now have the technology, the capability, to improve the standard of living of everyone on the planet.

He said we have the tools we need to move everyone up Maslow's pyramid of human consciousness. As we saw earlier, Maslow looked at humanity as forming a vast pyramid; at each level, we have different needs, and are at a different level of consciousness as a result.

The vast number of people on the bottom of the pyramid need food and shelter. Once these things are attained, you move up the pyramid, and your needs become security and health care and recovery. Once you've taken care of these needs, you move up the pyramid into the wonderful, expansive worlds of education.

This is where we learn to do our magic. When you educate people, you give them the tools to reach the top of the pyramid of human consciousness — *self-actualization*, to use Maslow's term. Fulfillment of their highest potential. Self-realization. Call it what you will.

Keep this in mind, always:

> **We have the technology to help everyone on earth
> move up the pyramid of human consciousness;
> all we lack is enough people using the technology
> to help themselves and others.**

More and more of us are using whatever technologies and resources are available to make this world a better place. A powerful wave of change is surging over the world — and it is change for good, for the highest good of all, if we keep affirming it.

It is self-evident that a primary purpose of every government on earth is to take care of its people, so that everyone has food, housing, security, and education. It's obvious that the only way this is achieved is for governments to work in partnership with their people. A great many successful countries know this already. Far too many countries, though, still don't have a clue.

How do we find solutions to the world's problems? This is a very good question to ask. Albert Einstein reminds us that the level of thinking that created the problems is incapable of realizing the solutions to the problems. The solutions have to come from a higher level of thinking.

How do we find the solutions? People are discovering solutions in a vast number of ways. For me, the writer and visionary who shows us how to find the solutions we need in the simplest, most effective way — a way I can grasp and use in my life every day — is Riane Eisler.

We looked at her work earlier, in our chapter on creating successful relationships. She sums it all up in her two great books, *The Chalice and the Blade* and *The Power of Partnership*: The essence of the problem lies in the model of domination and exploitation that is entrenched throughout the world, built on a need to control, and the solution lies in the model of partnership, built on respect for one another.

That's the single, simple key to making the dream work:

**The single key
to creating a world that works for all
is to work in partnership with *everyone*.
It's that simple.**

The world's problems are caused by domination and exploitation, with their underlying fear and need to control. The solutions are to be found by working in partnership, with underlying respect for each other — working together to dream of a world that works for all, to imagine how we can possibly achieve it, how we can work together to create it, taking one small step at a time.

MEDITATION FOR CREATING THE DREAM

Find a quiet place where you won't be disturbed, and get comfortable....

Take a slow, deep breath, and as you exhale, relax your body, from head to toe....
Take another deep breath, and as you exhale, relax your mind, let all thought go....
Take another deep breath, and let it all go....
Float in the ocean of your Presence....
Feel the energy of your Being....
It is life....
It is love....

From the formless space in front of you, let some forms emerge in your vast field of inner vision....
Imagine in some way a world that works for all....
Ask yourself, *How can we possibly create a world that works for all?*
See what images come to mind....

I see a vast number of people, peaceful armies of visionaries, artists, entrepreneurs, businesspeople, teachers, leaders, activists, and politicians all working together to build a new world.

We all hold the same vision, the same dream:

**It is possible to create a world
that works for all.**

We know we have the technology and the capability to house and feed and protect and educate everyone on the planet. Let's focus on this simple goal: *Let's create a world that works for all.*

We all realize that working in partnership is the only solution, and each one of us has our own unique contribution to make. What is yours?

Imagine a world that works for all....
What does it look like?
What is your *ideal scene* for the world?
What can you do to take steps toward realizing that dream?

What affirmation can you come up with that empowers that dream?
Maybe something like:

> **We are now creating
> a world that works for all,
> in partnership with everyone,
> in an easy and relaxed manner,
> a healthy and positive way,
> in its own perfect time,
> for the highest good of all.**

So be it. So it is!

Realizing the Dream

Millions of people already have the dream of creating a better world; millions of people are already doing great things. But there's so much more to do — and every one of us can do something. If you don't think you have the time, if you don't think you have the money, you can still pick up the trash around you as you walk somewhere. You can still recycle; you can still treat people nicely; you can still work in partnership with others.

Everyone can do something
to make the world a better place —
a world that works for all.

The Great Work ahead of us
is replacing the well-entrenched model of domination,
based on fear and a need to control,
with a new way of living,
a new model of partnership,
based on love and respect for all people
and all creation.

So be it. So it is!

Everyone can do something — so *do* something, now, today, or at least this week. We've got our work cut out for us. We need to house, feed, and educate everyone on the planet. We need to give everyone security and basic human rights, which means we need to bring an end to war, because war is a major violation of human rights. It's a big challenge, but it's doable. We have had the technology for years; the only thing we lacked was the vision. Now we have the vision: *We can create a world that works for all.*

What are you doing to help make the world a better place?

Every one of us can help. It doesn't matter who we are, whether we're rich or poor, optimist or pessimist. It doesn't matter what causes we identify with, what labels we use to describe ourselves. It doesn't matter whether we're conservative or liberal, religious or atheist, spiritual or pragmatic. We're all members of the same family, and we can all agree that there is plenty of room for improvement in the world.

The bad news is that the world is a mess. People are starving, homeless, and dying in wars. Far too many people are impoverished, hopeless, and dying from diseases that can be avoided.

The good news is that we can all do something about it. Every one of us can do something to improve our own lives and someone else's life as well. We can continue to discover more fully the brilliant power of partnership in our intimate and family relationships, our workplaces and communities, our nation, and our world. Along the way, we realize the great partnership we have with nature, and with spirit.

A World That Works for All

Let's imagine a world that works for all.

**There are four steps we can take:
dream, imagine, believe, and create.**

Let's dream of a world where everyone is respected and granted the basic human rights of life, liberty, and the pursuit of happiness. Let's dream of a world where everyone is housed and fed and educated; let's dream of a world where we are encouraged to dream and to live the life of our dreams.

Imagine the many ways — the limitless number of ways — that our dreams can be fulfilled.

Believe that it is possible. Who was it who said these powerful words?

**What we believe
we can achieve.**

If we can dream it, if we can imagine it clearly, we can create it.

We all have a Great Work ahead of us: the work of healing ourselves and our planet, creating a global self-sustaining system that supports life for all, for generation after generation, and helps everyone move up the pyramid of human consciousness into the realms of higher education and self-actualization.

So be it. So it is.

Thoughts for the 99 Percent
(and the 1 Percent as Well)

Some of this repeats what we've previously seen, but it's worth repeating things that are essential to our well-being.

Let's remember, always, Einstein's famous words — famous because his insight is brilliant enough to show us where to find the answers to all our problems:

**Significant problems cannot be solved
on the same level of thinking
that created the problems.**

What is the level of thinking that has caused most of our problems?

It's the *dominator model* that has been firmly entrenched around the world for the past three thousand years or so. It's a level of consciousness that is based on fear, the result of a set of deep underlying beliefs that the world is a hostile, difficult place and you have to fight for survival against enemies all around.

This level of consciousness creates endless problems, anger, resentment, and hostility, and all too often leads to violence, which of course leads to more violence — and, unless people break it by rising to a higher level of thinking and acting, we're trapped in an endless cycle of violence against one another.

Anger will not help solve problems; anger creates problems. Demonizing others will not help solve our problems; demonizing others causes problems. *Any* reaction that comes out of fear creates more problems than it solves. Any decision made while in fear is inevitably a bad decision.

The solution to our problems is not all that difficult to understand, though implementing it is a great challenge, because it involves changing our perceptions of ourselves and our world. We can find the solution only by moving into a higher level of consciousness, a higher level of thinking, based on love and respect rather than fear and a need to control. We can find the solution only by creating partnerships in which everyone is valued and gets what they need and deserve.

We've seen these words of Jesus before, and we'll see them again. Maybe someday we will be able to live them:

Love one another, as I have loved you.

Ramana Maharshi, one of the greatest teachers in India in the past century, summed it all up with these words:

The end of all wisdom is love,
love, love.

It's that simple. Love one another: That's the key to the solution of our problems. When we treat all others with love and respect, when we feel compassion for all of humanity, we can find solutions to the great global problems we face.

This I Believe

I believe there are far greater things in heaven and earth than we dream of in our philosophies.

I believe we are far greater beings than we dare imagine.

I believe we are here for a great purpose, no less than enlightenment, and, along the way, helping everyone on this planet evolve so that we're able to build a world of peace and prosperity for all.

I believe it is in the times of struggle when we find our greatest mental, physical, and spiritual strengths. It is in the times of turmoil when we find our spiritual path and forge the thoughts and tools necessary to bring us all to safety, peace, and light.

It is in the hardest times, the darkest times, when we find lasting inner peace.

I agree with Einstein: "There are only two ways to live your life. One is as though nothing is a miracle. The other is as though everything is a miracle. I choose the latter."

I believe all life is a miracle.

This beautiful planet we're on is a miraculous creation. Our lives are miracles.

Acknowledging and appreciating the miracle of your life — the miracle of *what is*, every moment of the day — lightens and brightens every moment.

I believe we're here to protect and serve our Mother Earth, so she may continue to be abundant and beautiful for thousands of generations.

I believe that war is murder, and murder is illegal, so war should be declared illegal by all nations who respect basic human rights to life, liberty, and the pursuit of happiness.

I believe in the power of partnership and negotiation:

The solution to all our problems is found as we learn to work together in partnership,

with love and respect for one another
and for the earth.

I believe a key to enlightenment and to the evolution of our species is this:

We're here to love and serve everyone,
including ourselves,
to help us all realize our dreams.

So be it. So it is!

To Sum It Up

There is a great value in keeping things simple, expressing things as briefly and concisely as possible, in the simplest words possible. To sum it up:

Love one another, as much as you can. At least realize that we're all human beings, and every one of us deserves respect. Every one of us deserves to be heard. Every one of us is entitled to life, liberty, and the pursuit of happiness.

Three things in human life are important.
The first is to be kind.
The second is to be kind.
And the third is to be kind.

— HENRY JAMES

Live and work in partnership as much as you can — the results are definitely worth it. Through the genius, power, and magic that emerges when we work in partnership, we can create a world that works for all.

> **If universal charity prevailed,**
> **Earth would be a heaven,**
> **and hell a fable.**
>
> — CHARLES COLTON

We can all give something — if not financially, we can give a bit of our time. And nearly all of us can give something financially, even if just a little bit. A little bit of money given by millions of people adds up to a powerful force for change.

We can all become part of the solution rather than part of the problem. What can you do? There are endless possibilities — and there is nothing more rewarding than doing your part in helping to create a world that works for all.

The Magical Key to a Heaven on Earth

When we dare to dream of a world that works for all, we inevitably dream of creating some kind of utopia. So many of the utopian dreams of the past had a major flaw: It was assumed that if the right external changes were made, an ideal society could be crafted.

Utopian dreams focused on the outer work necessary — and yet no utopian society will ever be created until we learn that the most essential work is internal, not external.

There is nothing new in this magical key. The great English writer John Milton said it over three hundred years ago in these powerful, simple words:

The mind is its own place, and in itself
Can make a Heaven of Hell, a Hell of Heaven.

The magical key to a heaven on earth is to be found within — in our own hearts and minds. Those of us raised in Christian traditions have heard it over and over:

The Kingdom of Heaven
is within.

There are an infinite number of paths that lead to peace, serenity, happiness, fulfillment — to heaven on earth.

Each one of these paths reveals to us in its own way that the key is within us, in our hearts and minds. We know in our hearts the next steps to take to continue our Great Work, and to evolve into higher and clearer levels of consciousness, culminating in self-actualization, self-realization, inner peace, and lightness.

So be it. So it is!

Be well.
Be in peace.

Appendix

Magical Passages

Copy these words and put them up on your wall. Carry them around with you. Email them to yourself.

Memorize some of them — not all of them, just a few. Take one that resonates with your heart, mind, and soul, and repeat it, over and over, so it's deeply imprinted in your subconscious mind.

**Do whatever is necessary
to imprint these words
in your vast, powerful subconscious mind.**

Prepare yourself for some truly magical, miraculous results.

So be it. So it is.

May we be guided by Spirit

every moment

in our thoughts, words, and actions.

And miracles will follow miracles,

and wonders will never cease,

because all our expectations

are for the highest good of all.

When you are inspired

by some great purpose,

some extraordinary project,

all your thoughts break their bonds.

Your mind transcends limitations,

your consciousness expands in every direction,

and you find yourself in a new, great,

and wonderful world.

Dormant forces, faculties, and talents become alive,

and you discover yourself to be a greater person by far

than you ever dreamed yourself to be.

— PATANJALI (ca. 250 BCE)

There is an ever-mysterious process of creation;

we can call it many things.

We will never understand how the process works,

but we can consciously set it in motion.

The tools we use are simply

our dreams and our imagination.

The Force of Life

Within every man and woman is a force

that directs and controls the entire course of life.

Properly used, it can heal every affliction

and ailment we may have.

— ISRAEL REGARDIE
The Art of True Healing

Ask and you will receive;

seek and you will find;

Knock, and the door will be opened to you.

— MATTHEW 7:7

Be at least as interested in what goes on

inside you as what happens outside.

If you get the inside right,

the outside will fall into place.

Primary reality is within, secondary reality without.

— ECKHART TOLLE
The Power of Now

Every day, in every way,

I am getting better and better,

in an easy and relaxed manner,

a healthy and positive way,

in its own perfect time,

for the highest good of all.

I am filled with healing energy.

I am healed, I am whole.

I am perfect as I am.

I close my eyes and see a field of light.

And I feel that light, and life,

in every cell of my body,

nurturing and healing every cell.

And I know that light, and life,

and love,

is who and what I am,

now and forever.

Amen.

This, or something better,

is now manifesting,

in totally satisfying and harmonious ways,

for the highest good of all.

So be it.

In the beginning was the word,

and the word was with God,

and the word was God....

In him was life;

and the life was the light of men.

— JOHN 1:4

Mind is the master power that molds and makes,
And we are Mind, and evermore we take
The tool of Thought, and, shaping what we will,
Bring forth a thousand joys, a thousand ills.
We think in secret, and it comes to pass —
Our world is but our looking glass.

— JAMES ALLEN
As You Think

I slept and dreamt
that life was joy
I woke and found
that life was service
I acted, and behold!
Service became joy

— RABINDRANATH TAGORE

I am sensible and in control of my finances;

I am creating total financial success,

in an easy and relaxed manner,

a healthy and positive way,

in its own perfect time,

for the highest good of all.

I do wonderful work

in a wonderful way

with wonderful people

for wonderful pay.

I live in a world of peace and plenty,

with abundance shared by all.

I help make this world a world that works for all,

where everyone on this sacred earth

is housed, fed, healed, and educated

so they can reach their greatest dreams.

Nature teaches me and guides me,

showing me how to live,

and how to become fully realized,

as powerful as a mountain,

as life giving as the sun.

⌇

Spirit flows through me every moment

with its healing energy.

I am guided by spirit, doing God's will.

I offer no resistance to life,

I am at peace with what is,

filled with grace, ease, and lightness.

Every moment, I feel my Being.

This is enlightenment.

⌇

The end of all wisdom

is love, love,

love!

— RAMANA MAHARSHI

There are only two ways to live your life.

One is as though nothing is a miracle.

The other is as though everything is a miracle.

I choose the latter.

— ALBERT EINSTEIN

All creation starts with a spiritual impulse,

then becomes a thought, then an emotion.

When thought and emotion are focused,

physical creation is the result.

A new law I give to you:

Love one another, as I have loved you.

— JESUS

Focus on your dreams with love,
and your dreams will soon become manifest.

Before long, you will be living in a world
that was only an insubstantial dream
a few years before.

I have omnipotence at my command
and eternity at my disposal.

— Eliphas Lévi

The day will come when,
after harnessing space,
the winds, the tides, and gravitation,
we shall harness for God the energies of love.
And, on that day, for the second time in the
history of the world,
we shall have discovered fire.

— Teilhard de Chardin

In an easy and relaxed manner,

in a healthy and positive way,

in its own perfect time,

for the highest good of all I pray

Spirit flows through me every moment

with its healing energy.

I am guided by spirit, doing God's will.

I offer no resistance to life,

I am at peace with what is,

filled with grace, ease, and lightness.

This is enlightenment.

In an easy and relaxed manner,

a healthy and positive way,

in its own perfect time,

for the highest good of all,

I am now creating the life and the world

of my dreams.

We are now living and working

together in partnership

to create a world that works for all.

So be it. So it is!

In an easy and relaxed manner,

in a healthy and positive way,

in its own perfect time,

for the highest good of all I pray

My marriage and family life and times alone

are sources of great joy,

grace, ease, and lightness.

I have plenty of time for family and friends,

and plenty of healing time for myself.

So be it. So it is.

You will become as great

as your dominant aspiration....

If you cherish a vision,

a lofty ideal in your heart,

you will realize it.

— James Allen
As You Think

To offer no resistance to life

is to be in a state of grace, ease,

and lightness.

— Eckhart Tolle
The Power of Now

The light of God surrounds me,

The love of God enfolds me,

The power of God flows through me,

And heals me, and protects me.

Wherever I am, God is,

And all is well.

The light of God surrounds us,

The love of God enfolds us,

The power of God flows through us,

And heals us, and protects us.

Wherever we are, God is,

And all is well.

If you can imagine it clearly enough,

it can become a reality,

in an easy and relaxed manner,

a healthy and positive way,

in its own perfect time,

for the highest good of all.

Love is the answer, love is the key.

It can open any door, give us eyes to see.

In our hearts lies a secret, and it sets us free —

all we need is love.

We are the creation of the forces of life,

an eternal blend of ecstasy and strife,

living as long as the universe stays,

which is forever, through our galaxies' nights and days.

From the big bang's beginning

to the black hole's destruction

is but a day in the life of our cosmic construction.

We'll live forever, we're the stuff of stars,

ever growing, ever changing,

born into this life, born into that,

changing this form for the one that comes next,

an eternal part of an eternal creation,

a quintessential piece of divine revelation!

You

are a unique

creative genius, capable

of realizing your most expansive

dreams in life and fulfilling your true purpose,

moving up, and helping others move up, the pyramid

of human consciousness to self-actualization and fulfillment.

And you shall decree a thing,

and it will be given unto you.

And light will shine upon your ways.

— JOB 22:28

What we are today comes from our thoughts of yesterday,

and our present thoughts build our life tomorrow;

our life is the creation of our mind.

— BUDDHA in the Dhammapada
(and JAMES ALLEN)

Prayer is the contact of your mind

with God-Mind,

in a way that shall result

in bringing to pass a desired good.

— ERNEST HOLMES

You will be what you will to be;

Let failure find its false content

In that poor word "environment,"

But Spirit scorns it, and is free.

It masters time, it conquers space,

It cows that boastful trickster Chance,

And bids the tyrant Circumstance

Uncrown, and fill a servant's place.

The human Will, that force unseen,

The offspring of a deathless Soul,

Can hew a way to any goal,

Though walls of granite intervene.

Be not impatient in delay,

But wait as one who understands;

When spirit rises and commands,

The gods are ready to obey.

— ELLA WHEELER WILCOX
(quoted by JAMES ALLEN in *As You Think*)

Within every adversity is the seed

of an equal or greater benefit.

Within every problem

is an opportunity.

Even in the knocks of life

we can find great gifts.

— Inspired by NAPOLEON HILL and
the Bhagavad Gita

First, we take a clear view of reality;

second, we identify what we hope for

in terms of the direction we'd like things to move in

or the values we'd like to see expressed;

and third, we take steps to move ourselves or our

situation in that direction.

— JOANNA MACY and CHRIS JOHNSTONE
Active Hope

When you imagine the Magician within you,
you summon the creative force of the universe
to do what you will.

❧

The human opportunity, the religions tell us,
is to transform our flashes of insight
into abiding light.

— HUSTON SMITH

❧

Underneath the level of physical appearances
and separate forms,
you are one with all that is.

— ECKHART TOLLE
The Power of Now

I am a visionary, a magician;

I am now creating the life of my dreams,

in an easy and relaxed manner,

a healthy and positive way,

in its own perfect time,

for the highest good of all.

My marriage and family life

are filled with grace, ease, and lightness.

So be it. So it is.

What is the Purpose of a Family?

To protect and support each one of us,

To be in partnership together,

To respect and love and listen to each other,

To encourage each other to be happy and healthy,

And to help us all fulfill our highest dreams.

Gratitude for the present moment

and the fullness of life now

is true prosperity.

— ECKHART TOLLE
The Power of Now

⁓

We will never understand the forces of creation.

But we can set them in motion —

and then sit back in wonder

at the mystery and majesty of it all.

⁓

Make no little plans;

they have no magic to stir your blood....

Make big plans;

aim high in hope and work.

— DANIEL BURNHAM
Architect and urban planner

I am guided by spirit

every moment.

I am guided by spirit

to find and fulfill

my calling, my vocation.

I am guided by spirit

to grow into my potential,

and realize the life of my dreams.

So be it. So it is!

Our thoughts and prayers of today

determine our life in the future.

Dare to dream and affirm the highest,

most wonderful life you can imagine.

Keep the dream, the vision, in mind:
It is possible to create a world that works for all,
where all are fed, housed, and educated.
This is the Great Work ahead of us.

Since everything is an illusion,
perfect in being what it is,
having nothing to do with good or bad,
or whether we accept it or reject it,
one may well burst out in laughter.

— LONG CHEN PA
The Natural Freedom of Mind

Never doubt that a small group
of thoughtful, committed people
can change the world.
Indeed, it is the only thing that ever has.

— MARGARET MEAD

If universal charity prevailed,

Earth would be a heaven,

and hell a fable.

— CHARLES COLTON

Three things in human life are important.

The first is to be kind.

The second is to be kind.

And the third is to be kind.

— HENRY JAMES

The mind is its own place, and in itself

Can make a Heaven of Hell, a Hell of Heaven.

— JOHN MILTON

We are now creating

a world that works for all,

working in partnership with all of humanity,

in an easy and relaxed manner,

a healthy and positive way,

in its own perfect time,

for the highest good of all.

The happiness that is derived from some secondary source

is never very deep.

It is only a pale reflection of the joy of Being,

the vibrant peace that you find within

as you enter the state of nonresistance.

Being takes you beyond the polar opposites of the mind

and frees you from dependency on form.

Even if everything were to collapse

and crumble all around you,

you would still feel a deep inner core of peace.

You may not be happy,

but you will be at peace.

— ECKHART TOLLE
The Power of Now

We are now a vital force,

a great wave of visionaries, artists, teachers,

entrepreneurs, businesspeople, and leaders

who are transforming not only our own lives

but the whole world as well,

creating a world that works for all,

in an easy and relaxed, healthy and positive way,

in its own perfect time,

for the highest good of all.

So be it. So it is.

Be well.

Be in peace.

Acknowledgments

This work owes much to many. It was Israel Regardie's great little book *The Art of True Healing* that set me on the magical path. Katsuki Sekida's instruction to the beauty of Zen, as well as his great work *Two Zen Classics*, helped me let go of a lot of the anxiety, doubts, and fears that seemed nearly overwhelming at times. And it was in the weekend workshop with Ken Keyes Jr., author of *Handbook to Higher Consciousness*, that I discovered how to examine and change so many of my deeply held beliefs.

James Allen's little masterpiece *As You Think* helped me set my course, and a weekend studying what was then called Silva Mind Control (and is now called Silva Mind Body Healing — a much better name!) gave me some of the magical tools in this book, including finding my Inner Sanctuary and Inner Guide.

Thanks to Buckminster Fuller, Riane Eisler, and Barbara Marx Hubbard for their vision and guidance. They have helped me come to understand that it is entirely possible to create a world that works for all.

Thanks to Kristen Cashman and Mark Colucci for their excellent editing work. This book is far better because of their contributions. Thanks to everyone at New World Library and Publishers Group West for their wonderful work in publishing this book and getting it out into the world.

And finally, to my wife, Aurilene: thanks for your love and support, and for giving me the time and space I need to do projects like this. And to my son, Kai: You have given me so much more than you'll ever realize (unless someday you're blessed with a child of your own).

This book is dedicated to everyone who is open-minded enough to actually read it, and to everyone who has taken my courses. Thanks for your love and appreciation and, best of all, your never-ending miracle stories.

About the Author

Marc Allen is an internationally renowned author and speaker. His books, audios, and seminars have been life-changing experiences for a great many people.

He cofounded New World Library (with Shakti Gawain in 1977, and has guided the company from a small start-up to its current position as one of the leading independent publishers in the country. He is the author of several books, including *The Greatest Secret of All*, *The Millionaire Course*, and *Visionary Business*. He has produced several audio projects as well, including *Stress Reduction and Creative Meditations* and a complete course of audio downloads, *Success With Ease: Creating the Life of Your Dreams.*

He is also an accomplished composer and musician, and has recorded several albums of music. For more information about Marc Allen and his seminars and teleconferences, go to www.MarcAllen.com. For more on his publishing company, go to www.NewWorldLibrary.com. To sample his music, check out www.WaterCourseMedia.com.

James Allen, As You Think
Psycal Bagahdie, The Art of
Sure Healing

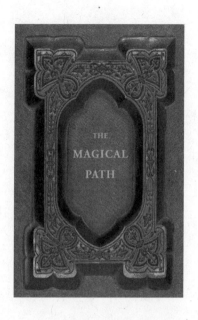

New World Library
has produced a special hardcover limited edition
of only 500 copies,
numbered and signed by the author.

The price for this treasure is $50.00.

To order a copy,
contact New World Library at
800-972-6657.